CALL ME A DOCTOR

Tales of six medical men who went
elsewhere and did other things

Jack Griffitts, M.D.

The American Spectator
Arlington • Virginia

Published by The American Spectator
P.O. Box 549
2020 N. 14th Street
Arlington, Virginia 22216-0549

Illustrations by Elliott Banfield

Manufactured in the United States of America

First Edition

91-070373
Library of Congress Cataloging-in-Publication Data
Griffitts, Jack, 1912—
Call me a doctor: tales of six medical men who went elsewhere and
did other things/Jack Griffitts.
p.   cm.
Includes bibliographical references.
1. United States—Biography. 2. Physicians—United States-
Biography. 3. South Africa—Biography. 4. Physicians—South
Africa—Biography. I. Title.
CT215.G75 1991   610'.92'2—dc20
[B]

ISBN 0-9629072-0-0

To my colleagues,
Bewitched, Bebothered and Bewildered.
Hang in there.

Table of Contents

I'LL WAIT FOR YOU   1
James D. Long, M.D.
1793 - 1822

WASHINGTON IRVING'S "GENERAL VON POOFENBERG"   47
James Wilkinson, M.D.
1757-1825

GENTEEL FILIBUSTER   79
William Walker, M.D.
1824 - 1860

AN UNLIKELY RAIDER   121
Leander Starr Jameson
1853 - 1917

A VERY INSUBORDINATE MAN   157
Leonard A. Wood, M.D.
1860 - 1927

A LIAR AND A GENTLEMAN   197
Frederick A. Cook, M.D.
1865 - 1940

FOREWORD

A bit more than a generation ago, the entertainer Woody Woodbury, a fatigue cap on the back of his head, smiled sadly, and stopped fiddling with his piano long enough to say, "I know a lot more old smokers and drinkers than I do old Doctors." I assume he meant well, that doctors worked themselves out before their times had come.

I recall (dimly) seeing two white-helmeted policemen astride their black Harley-Davidson motorcycles. I expected them to zoom the motors and take off with sirens screaming, as usual. But they started, side by side, slowly making a right turn, matching the quiet sliding motion of a big gray Cadillac with its extended box-like body and its silver plated sign, "Roberts Funeral Home." I did not stay to count the cars that followed, all with headlights on, which spoke with ridiculous weakness to the bright midday sun. The procession was long. Who had so many friends out at noon on a Tuesday workday?

The Riverland News said he was Charles "Woody" Perkins, M.D., age 68. "He delivered half the people in this town," Mrs. Howie Gibson, 65, said, with a quiver in her voice. "And more of them who got ready for school got their shots from him. If he wasn't sitting up at night by a bed, he was scrubbing to help take an appendix out of a young belly. I swear there never was a man like him to be at the beck and call of everybody."

People are in so much motion these days, being born in one place, schooled in others, married away from home, and work-

i

ing and dying in so many locations that the idea of the population of a town being handled from birth by one doctor no longer fits. Yet, most doctors do practice their professions to a ripe age. Most become a part of the communities in which they live. Their wives and children need them for church, the PTA, City Hall meetings, and at the Country Club. This breed of man usually accepts the role of special member of his community, delivers the product of his profession (the obstetrical leaning of a pun is not intended) and goes to his reward amid a throng of grieving beneficiaries of his services. Old movies (and TV reruns) in black and white gave us Jean Hersholt sitting at the bedside of a stricken child awaiting the crisis, hair disheveled, jacket aside, collar open, tie askew, holding the hand of the frantic mother. Dr. Kildare and his boss, Dr. Marcus Welby, Dr. Ben Casey and all the predecessors of General Hospital and St. Elsewhere (in living color) have shown doctors at their trade, and most often favorably. Many thanks!

With his years of special study and training the doctor has learned where pain comes from and how to help it go away. He knows the fright of a wound and how to help to fix it. He knows the joys of life and shares them. He knows travail and the need for comfort. He knows the physiology of the too-short life and the certainty of passing back to the earth. He can, and often does, earn the love and affection that may be attested to only by the length of his funeral procession.

The lives of most doctors fill the people's needs without the fame, notoriety, or attention given to stage performers, and they are passed over in the annals of history. There have been many, however, who left their profession and made lasting impressions in other walks of life. There is, of course, no law or reason against changing one's mind at any station of life on the journey from zygotic union to the final urn. Often as I discover a character in a book to have been a physician I detour long enough to chase down the cause of his turn from medical life. As would be expected, the tide of events of his day has a telling impact on his change of vocation.

Of the many who wandered, I have chosen to present but a few. In the field of human behavior I would love to tell you about Saint Luke, how he became a doctor, and of his doctoring life. I couldn't find the records and, uncharacteristically, I dared not fictionalize the life of the beloved Apostle. I wish I had the mind and talent to bring you Doctor Paracelsus (also known as Theophrastus Bombastus von Hohenheim) in a short essay. That old man has confused generations and completely discouraged me from trying to explain his complicated teachings.

High in the esteem of mankind are doctors who have commented on human behavior and thus influenced modern society. Sir Thomas Browne and John Locke found the time and means to give us guidance while at the same time caring for patients and making scientific contributions to society. And in our own time, Albert Schweitzer, M.D., first famous in music and philosophy, later was acclaimed for his humane clinical work in Africa's deepest forests.

The names of many doctors are inscribed in American history. Four were signers of the Declaration of Independence: Josiah Bartlett and Matthew Thornton of New Hampshire, Benjamin Rush of Pennsylvania, and Lyman Hall of Georgia. Joseph Warren, M.D. was an early martyr, falling at the Battle of Bunker Hill. James McHenry, M.D. was an early Secretary of War, whose name was given to the Fort over which the Star Spangled Banner "so proudly waved." In North Carolina, Doctor Ephraim Brevard penned the dubious Mecklenberg Declaration which antedated Mr. Jefferson's more lasting document. Henry Dearborn, M.D. was in the military longer, perhaps, than any other general in United States history (1775-1816) and was twice Secretary of War, Ambassador to Portugal, etc. His fellow physician, William Eustis, served with him and was also a Secretary of War in those times. Thomas Mercer, M.D. of New Jersey fell while leading New Jersey troops against the British. Doctor Thomas Walker of Virginia led settlers into Kentucky in Daniel Boone's time. Doctor Marcus Whitman gave his life to the establishment of the Oregon Territory.

The talent for creating poetry and writing prose has overcome credit for the application of medical knowledge in an impressive number of literary stars. Doctor John Keats[1] could have, and maybe did, treat physical disorders in his friends, Byron and Shelley (those lovers). The time to write Oliver Wendell Holmes's *Autocrat at the Breakfast Table* came after he had fulfilled his regular duties to practice and teach medicine at Dartmouth College and Harvard University. He led his American associates in the prevention of infections during the birthing process. Anton Chekhov went to the heart of the Russian kulak with his pen, a stethoscope hanging from his neck. The poet-pediatrician, William Carlos Williams, could not get away from his Paterson, N.J. practice because his poems didn't bring in enough money. Doctor Sir Arthur Conan Doyle delivered the tales of Sherlock Holmes through his alter-ego, Dr. Watson. Somerset Maugham buried his medical ambitions in a flair of literary achievement. Even today we have been enriched by the genius of Walker Percy, whose medical career was interrupted shortly after he graduated at Columbia-Presbyterian in New York. And haven't we been blessed by the novels of Frank Slaughter, Michael Crichton, Ferrol Sams, and A. J. Cronin, to name a few? Or, if you simply wanted words rather than sumptuously prepared literary feasts, try the Thesaurus of Doctor Peter Mark Roget.

In the political arena there have been numerous Congressmen who have given their time to governmental functions.

More fame has been achieved in foreign lands. The first Governor of South Africa in the sixteenth century was a ship's surgeon, Heinrich von Riebeeck. In more recent times we have a University of Michigan graduate in medicine, "Papa Doc" Duvalier, who practiced political surgery in Haiti. In nearby Cuba, the Argentine medical guerrilla, Che Guevara, shone briefly before his assassination in Bolivia. The communist, Salvador Allende, M.D. had a career in Chile, shortened, they say, by North American interests. And, as I write, Doctor Jonas Savimbi tries to rid Angola of the invasion of Marxism and Cuban soldiers.

On hot, humid days air conditioning's presence should remind us of the Florida doctor, John Gorrie, who invented an ice-making machine in 1850 to cool his feverish patients. He never got done with his struggles to enforce his patents. A good friend and neighbor of Dolly Madison's, Doctor William Thornton, stammered badly but had the talent to design the Capitol Building in Washington, being built in Madison's time. And, in what category could we put Armand Hammer, M.D.? He made decisions that Wall Street listened to, and dealt with Moscow's top people, whom no other American could have begun to approach.

The six doctors I write about (like Plutarch, I just want to tell about their lives, not write history) had outstanding human traits. They were intelligent, impulsive, brave, daring, and somehow wrong, each of them. Had they stayed in the harness to which they had been trained, they could have served well any patient who called them. Having heard a different call, they wandered. They took with them strong commitments to their new causes, maybe stronger than their first drive to become doctors.

To the many scholars who have given us the biographical details from which my borrowings come, I give my sincerest thanks. And where sources were thin I took the liberty of listening to my imagination. For any offenses from that source, I apologize.

James J. Griffitts, M.D.

Beau Bois

Dunnellon, Florida, 1990

[1]I went to a University librarian to look up Keats. Actually he did wear a plastic green eye-shade held by an elastic band around his blond, balding pate. He could have been Scrooge's apprentice clerk, the looks of him seedy, baggy pants, rumpled shirt, and all. His tie had to go back to the '50s at least, skinny and twisted into a slouchy gathering just missing the center cleave of his collar. He must have been born a denizen of a demon's library.

"Do you have a collection of biographies of English authors?" I asked.

"Of course. What are you looking for?" He resented my intrusion into his day.

"Keats. I want to look up his medical training. . . ." I was interrupted as he scowled, saying, "Keats was not a doctor."

Standing on a narrow ladder, he took a book from a series high in the rack. He handed me the tall tome which he had opened at 'Keats, John' with no comment.

Sure enough, in the first few lines I found that Keats had apprenticed in a pharmacy, then studied and qualified as a physician. I didn't tarry. I thanked the man and left, feeling the pleasant flush of having at least once proved smarter than a superior library person.

I'LL WAIT FOR YOU

James D. Long, M.D.
1793 - 1822

CHAPTER ONE

Had not Andrew Jackson been in hot pursuit of Jesse Hart Benton on that steamy morning in September 1813, Nashville's Young James Long might have been spared an early grave in the non-Catholic section of a cemetery in Chapultepec, Mexico City. It came about, this wise.

In the young State of Tennessee, Andrew Jackson had been its first representative to the Union. He returned to Nashville as a presiding Judge, yet he was known to be a man easy to rile, especially with regard to his wife, Rachel. He had seemingly settled the matter with his part-time co-husband, Jason Hobards, and had laid one detractor to rest with his acknowledged skill with a pistol. As he judged, farmed, managed slaves, speculated in land, raised horses, bet on races, cockfights and most anything gamey, he was also the leader of the Tennessee militia. He got his nickname, old Hickory, for leading them to Natchez to meet a British threat on orders from General James Wilkinson (the next doctor told of in these accounts.) The threat was real only in Wilkinson's imagination. Jackson and the Tennesseans had to make a weary return up the Natchez Trace. Giving up his mount to a disabled hillbilly, Jackson, on foot, was seen to be as tough "as a hickory

nut." The experience ripened the feeling of Colonel William
Carroll and John Coffee for their leader. It also put Jackson on
the opposite side of Wilkinson forever. (This was later noted
in Aaron Burr's trial when Jackson supported him against
Wilkinson's charges.)

The Tennessee militia continued to function in weekly
meetings. At the officer's mess Colonel Carroll upbraided a
young officer for ungentlemanly conduct. Proving Carroll's
point, the young officer challenged his Commander to a duel.
Carroll, a haughty one, declined on the basis that his challenger
was not a gentleman. (It seems that there were many ways to
avoid the shooting—like, "You're not a citizen of this State,"
or, "You make me so sick I cannot appear.") In this case, the
matter stayed alive, as another offended officer, Jessie Benton,
stepped in place and said, "Try me, sir. I am a gentleman, and
I demand satisfaction."

Carroll then needed a second, and who better than his
staunch friend, the pistol-experienced Judge Jackson. 'Old
Hickory' tried to talk Carroll out of the match and used his
political savvy with Thomas Hart Benton (a fellow politician
and brother to Jessie) to cancel the affair. Both parties refused
to give in and the duel was fought in the hours of dawn in the
Nashville woods.

Under the *Code Duello* they fought with pistols at eight
paces. By cowardly design or accident, Benton stooped down
as he fired, wounding Carroll in the shoulder. Carroll's deliberate shot tore a sizeable patch out of the seat of Jessie's
britches and the cheek of his ass.

The halls and porches of Nashville taverns buzzed, tittered,
and guffawed at the doubly wounded Benton. He wrote his
brother, "That hoss's ass, Jackson, him sitting out there at the
Heritage snickering."

Thomas Hart Benton, as easy to rile as Andrew Jackson was, was fiery. He wrote to Jackson berating him for becoming involved in this quarrel. "You, sir, have done dishonor to your position on the bench."

This did it for the Judge. He promised Thomas Benton, "I will have a horsewhip to hand when I see you, and I shall thrash you as you deserve."

Six weeks later, September 4, 1813, Jesse, now healed, and Thomas Hart Benton, took their saddle bags into the City Hotel. Across the Courthouse Square Jackson, John Coffee, and Andrew Donelson, Jackson's nephew, came into the street from breakfast at the Nashville Inn. They crossed the Square, passed the Post Office, and approached the Hotel. Jackson saw Benton and brandished his whip; Benton reached for his pistol, and backed into the doorway of the Hotel.

As Jackson moved from the porch to follow Thomas Benton, Jessie, concealed behind the door, shot Jackson in the left shoulder, knocking him to the floor. Thomas fired twice at Jackson's falling form, neither bullet finding its mark. Jessie was prevented from shooting again by Donelson, who tried to put Jessie on his sword blade, which broke on a heavy button. Jessie pulled the trigger of his pistol, aimed at Donelson's side, but it failed to fire. The giant, Coffee, came through the doorway blazing away at Thomas Hart Benton, who, stepping back, fell down a flight of stairs, thus saving his badly bruised body from certain death. The Three Stooges, at their best, could not have staged a duel more comically, except, of course, Andrew Jackson lay badly wounded.

Dr. Holland and young James Long rushed Jackson to a bed in the Inn. They staunched the massive hemorrhage, spouting from a torn artery behind the humerus of Jackson's left shoulder. It was necessary to open wide the shoulder wound to ligate the bleeding vessel. Doctors Holland, Boggs, and young Long obeyed 'Old Hickory' as he forbade amputation. Rachel, badly upset, nursed him back to an early partial recovery. After ten days at the Inn, they returned to the Hermitage. This wound remained a problem for Jackson for more than five years. He was already carrying a slug of lead in scar tissue near his heart, the relic of the duel seven years before that had put young Dickinson in his grave.

War, not wanted by the Eastern States, but urged by Clay, Calhoun and the Westerners, had come. In the South, war-like activity was being carried out, mostly by the Indians with the connivance of the British. News came of an Indian massacre of almost three-hundred settlers at Fort Mims in Mississippi Territory. This was the work of William Weatherford (Red Eagle), the seven-eighths white nephew of the Creek leader, Alexander MacGilvray. Madison ordered Jackson to lead a punitive expedition into the Creek nation. James Long went with Carroll's militia as an adjunct surgeon. He kept close to Dr. Samuel Hogg, Jackson's surgeon, and in Jackson's tent twice a day he helped the determined General to remove his arm from the sling, and then from his epauleted jacket and red undershirt. Every third day some of the proud flesh had to be cut from the open wound. At those times the General put his pipe aside and took generous gulps of Tennessee whiskey.

Jackson's problems were two-fold. The Indians did not play the game of mass encounter, but rather the guerrilla tactics of 'hit and run.' Jackson's militia was not well-disciplined, and waiting to fight wore thin their soldiering. Jackson had to show his toughness in keeping the men from deserting. The arrival of army regulars from East Tennessee came in time to reinforce Jackson's plans to meet Weatherford in force at Horseshoe Bend in the Tallapoosa River.

In December 1813, at Fort Strother, Jackson was ready. Dr. Hogg and his surgeons, including James Long, had more than 100 ill soldiers, most of them victims of dysentery. Ensign Sam Houston came in with extensive wounds of his chest. Long cleaned and bandaged him so he could return and later incur damage to both his legs that almost ended the career of the young Raven.

Jackson's forces moved toward the Horseshoe Bend. A small group of Coffee's foragers had fallen into a Creek ambush. Dr. Long joined four militiamen in a buck wagon carrying extra rifles and ammunition. A scout led them to the tree-lined scene of the ambush. It was almost dark. The captive blue-suited Coffee men could be seen huddled, apparently bound to each other and to small saplings. Long, shrieking, half in fun and half in terror, took off in the wagon, the militia men firing. Surprise was complete, two Indian guards were downed, and the rest fled. The party, including those rescued, returned in less than an hour after leaving camp.

That evening, while Long changed the dressings on Andrew Jackson's left shoulder, the grim old soldier said, "Doctor Jimmy, what in hell do you mean, leaving the sick and wounded?"

"Sir." The young surgeon was half afraid he'd see the vaunted wrath of Old Hickory. "I only left them for a little while—a moment."

"I don't want you to get used to shooting, son. They's enough of us. We need good doctors more'n we need good shooters. See that you take care of our skin and bones. There'll be time for you to do other things."

"Yes, Sir." James grinned; he liked the praise, faint as it was, from such a leader.

On March 27, 1814 at Horseshoe Bend, Andrew Jackson destroyed the Creek Nation. Surrender terms were proffered, but the 'red sticks' of Red Eagle shot at the messengers. Forty Indians were taken prisoner, the rest killed. One half of the dead bodies were in the river. Jackson lost 49, with 150 wounded.

John Reid, Jackson's secretary, told the tale of Red Eagle's surrender and his vow to have the Creeks live in peace. Weatherford walked off into the fog of history.

James Long got back to Nashville in April 1814. Doctors Holland and Hogg empaneled a review board, and a degree and license to practice medicine was granted to the handsome uniformed twenty-one-year-old Tennessean. His father and two brothers, standing by, were rightfully proud.

CHAPTER TWO

The Constitution of the new Union was but six years old when James Long was born in 1793 in Culpeper County, Virginia. His father, Jonathan, like many veterans of the War of Independence from England, moved on toward the seemingly endless western boundaries of the seaboard States, seeking land and better chances than to compete with landed and ingrained old timers of the east. As the Army, under Wayne, Tyler and Harrison, discouraged the Indians, more settlers came over the Allegheny and Blue Ridge mountains and through the Cumberland Gap to Kentucky and around the Great Smokies into Tennessee.

Jonathan, after a stay in Kentucky, took his young family into 'Nolichucky John' Sevier's new Tennessee settlement near the Cumberland river, where James Robertson's village, Nashville, was beginning to bloom. His boys were schooled at a private academy. They spent some part of each day attending to duties in Jonathan's general merchandise store. James seemed headed for a career in trading, except that his very closest adult friend was Doctor William Holland. He worked hard, saved money, dressed neatly, and met and made friends with the people of his town as he delivered purchases made at the store.

James missed no chance to hitch Dr. Holland's black bay to the two-wheeled buggy. In 1809 he moved into a loft over the doctor's office and began to read the doctor's books. He assisted in operations, he dressed wounds, he wiped the horse down, and he kept office while the doctor found some relaxation in Talbot's Tavern or wherever there might be a card game.

After two years, Dr. Holland got the boy a place in the Transylvania Medical College in Lexington, Kentucky. This was 'the' school in the West, its fame due to the presence of Daniel Drake, who was determined to make it the equal of medical schools in Philadelphia and New York. James attended lectures in anatomy, the workings of the body, the virtues of herbs and medicines, aids to birthing, the cupping and bleeding of the sick, and treatment of disease of the bowel that so tortured the west. He returned to Nashville in February 1813, a cultured young man of twenty, ready to try for his license. A few months later he was a part of Tennessee's war effort.

CHAPTER THREE

News of Jackson's success in the Creek Nation in 1814 thrilled a somewhat despondent Washington. Even peace-demanding Yankee Easterners noted the new military figure, Jackson. But the mood was pessimistic. In the early summer Napoleon turned tail for Elba. The British in America took on new zest. Pushing the Navy out of the way in the Chesapeake, they put a force ashore and finally burned the White House and most of Washington. The British laid plans to apply the finishing touch to the American upstarts. "After Napoleon, what are a bunch of dirty-shirts?"

Jackson took his assignment seriously, embarrassing a more timid Washington. He moved southward into Georgia, Florida and southern Alabama, neutralizing Indian threats, and making it difficult for the British to make a land effort in the area. What had appeared to be a future British stronghold in the Mobile area was dismantled. He correctly guessed at a major effort to be launched at New Orleans. He arrived there in December 1814, promptly arranging for the defense of the approaches to that important city, heard of the pirates of Barataria, but refused to grant them amnesty for their past offenses against the people. He had trees cut down to block the many bayou approaches to the city. He got the local support of fancy-dressed 'militia' and from Wilkinson's U. S. troops in nearby Mississippi. He ordered the loyal Tennessee giant, John Coffee, to march the Tennessee Regulars to New Orleans. He got John Adair to bring two thousand Kentuckians down the Mississippi on their keelboats. Carroll's brigade, disobeying orders, loaded barges on the Cumberland river at Nashville. Among them were Doctors Samuel Hogg and James Long, who were familiar with the Commanding General's still draining left shoulder. Finally, Jackson, needing all the help he could get, yielded and accepted Jean Lafitte, his men and their cannons.

In three weeks a big general, Coffee, on a tall Tennessee thoroughbred arrived at the head of a column of weary, coonskin-hatted, woolen clad roughnecks, armed with hunting knives, rifles, and tomahawks stuck in their belts. They had walked the Natchez Trace again. A few hours later, Carroll and his well-rested men arrived. They had come by flatboats and on the way from Nashville had luckily acquired more than a thousand extra rifles and ammunition. James Long had gone ashore at Natchez and after a roaring night partying, "Under the Hill," had slept like a prince at a clean inn on the higher side of the lovely village.

Jackson breathed a sigh of relief, forgiving the sharp and capable Carroll who had disobeyed his orders by coming in boats. He got news that the British forces were approaching through Lake Borgne; they landed in force on the Villere Plantation about eight miles east of the city. Jackson attacked the British after sunset on that dark, gloomy night. Coffee's slightly rested men could hardly show off their vaunted marksmanship in the cold, ghoulish night. After the British doused their campfires, only barrages from the *USS Carolina* on the Mississippi river afforded light enough for men to see at whom

they fired. The British, under the command of the Earl of
Pakenham, were seasoned soldiers. In military circles the Earl
was held to be the equal of Napoleon's conqueror, the Duke of
Wellington. Even so, a seasoned British officer spoke well of
his opponents, Coffee's sweaty ones. "In the whole course of
my military career, I remember no scene like this. The American officer whose sword I demanded, damned well nearly cut
my head off." The battle was indecisive; Jackson ordered a
withdrawal. Losses on both sides were heavy. A prisoner
taken by one of Coffee's lieutenants proved to be a Major
Samuel Mitchell, who was supposed to have set fire to the
Capitol in Washington.

Jackson prepared a defensive line behind the Rodriguez
Canal, a twenty foot wide ditch. There were barricades in front
of and behind bales of cotton. The defensive line extended
well out into a cypress swamp on the left beyond a wide, flat
sugar cane field. On the right the barricade ended on the levee
of the Mississippi river. Lafitte placed his batteries on the left
between Carroll and Coffee, whose men took the tough duty in
the swamp.

Jackson had about five thousand troops behind the barricades and in front of his headquarters, the double balconied
McCarte plantation house. The second story bedroom had a
good view of the battlefield before it. The *USS Louisiana* lay
down river from the *Carolina*. Her Naval guns were an important part of Jackson's artillery. To see her floating on the river,
higher than the porch, was a strange but welcome sight.

On Christmas day, James Long assisted in dressing
Jackson's shoulder. He and Dr. Hogg shared a Christmas toast
with Old Hickory, drinking large glasses of good New Orleans
brandy. The old soldier later blew out his candle, and slept
eight hours uninterrupted; the best sleep he'd had in weeks,

maybe months.[1] Unknown to him, and to many, five thousand miles away in Ghent, Belgium, American and British diplomats signed a treaty of peace. There was, of course, no radio, no satellite, no news, no ceasefire.

On December 30, British naval guns, now on land, destroyed the pesky *Carolina*. A few of the *Carolina* cannon were moved by Dominick You, the erstwhile buccaneer, to his battery just in front of Carroll's brigade on the far left.

On the cold and foggy morning of January 1, 1815, Jackson hoped for a day of peace. He invited New Orleans politicians and a few ladies to come out to the plantation back of McCarte's for a display of the Army. A small Creole military band played a peppy martial air. Suddenly, the heavy cannon of Pakenham's fleet, brought ashore with much labor, belched a thundering explosion. The west end of the roof of the McCarte's plantation house flew in every direction. One visitor, a Mississippi politician, Charles Poindexter,[2] was knocked from his feet. He landed in the lap of a young negro field hand who was crouched against the downstairs plaster wall of the kitchen. The heavy man struck his head on the wall as he fell. The picture of a fat, crying man, sitting in the lap of a much smaller and very black boy, was surely ludicrous. It soon became evident that the youngster had lost the back of his skull and was dead.

Dr. Long, alerted at the first cannonade, rushed to his battle post in Carroll's sector. He found Dominick You, half-covered with cotton from a ruptured bale, on his hands and knees, blinded from a wound, hunting the placement of his cannon. Long took him to his battle station, washed out his eyes, and looked for injuries. You had received a heavy blow to his inner right thigh and had developed a hematocele in the left part of his scrotum. Long placed a belt of soft cloth around his waist and with one of Dominick's own bandanas, fashioned a cod-piece to bear the swollen part until he might find some other use for it. Dominick was grateful, and limped back to his cannon.

The next event of the day was an artillery duel. The Americans, especially those on the *Louisiana*, gave better than they took. By late afternoon on New Year's day it was apparent that the Americans held artillery supremacy. Dominick You, aching or not, received a special Jackson citation for his performance.

Pakenham, suspecting that Jackson's left near the Cypress swamp was the weakest spot, dispatched an infantry move on Coffee's area. Long left his post to go with a crack platoon from Carroll's brigade. They turned the British back. Jackson, watching the artillery exchange from the second balcony, also saw the slight bending of and the response in Coffee's line. Later in the bedroom, Long was alone with the General and his secretary, John Reid. As the General took off his tunic, he growled, "Jimmy, I saw you this afternoon. You just won't listen to me, will you?"

"General Jackson, I knew there would be some wounded Carroll men and I wanted to be close by."

"I don't believe a word you say, boy. You just damn well want to be a soldier, like old James McHenry, or even worse, Henry Dearborn. They probably would have been pretty good doctors if they had stayed, but they're sorry generals. Stick by your training. You hear me?"

"Yes, Sir!"

After the New Year's day test of artillery strength, Pakenham decided to wait on reinforcements via Lake Borgne. As he regrouped his forces, Jackson was elated by the arrival, finally, of John Adair and 2,250 militiamen from Kentucky.

Many of them wore rags from the hard journey. Less than twenty percent had arms, but Carroll's extra supplies helped. The Kentuckians lined up in Carroll's rear and to the right of Coffee's men. They were welcome.

Old Hickory was up at one a.m. on January 8, 1815, restless and feeling that, "this is the day." The coffeepot was hot, and after two cups, he lighted his pipe, bundled up against the cold, and went out to inspect the lines from river to swamp. He bantered with those of the polyglot group who were awake—Louisiana dandies, Santo Domingo black free men, Mississippi farmers, some old Napoleon veterans and their French leader, Kentuckians, Tennesseans, even pirates from Barataria. Many slept lightly at their positions, huddled and blanketed against the damp cold.

At daylight a rocket flared to signal an attack by the fine troops who had bested the great Napoleon. The best of England, far from home, would show off the most disciplined infantrymen in the world. They marched in close formation and were met at a distance by accurate gap-making American artillery fire. They came on into range of the Tennessee and Kentucky sharpshooters, who would fire a volley and step back to reload. In the meantime they were replaced by another hundred or so, who came up ready to fire. First General Gibbs, then the Earl of Pakenham, and the colonel of the gallant kilted Highlanders, fell, mortally wounded. And still England's finest came.

The action lasted two hours. The cream of England lay on the stubby cane fields. Estimates ranged from 2,500 to 3,000 British deaths. The Americans lost 7 killed, and but 6 wounded. Andrew Jackson, never noted for religious fervor, was heard to say, "The unerring hand of Providence shielded my men."

the spine of one Alex Ferguson. He paused to give the man a small glass of brandy.

At this moment, on the wide balcony which surrounded the second floor of the Propinquity mansion, a teenage black girl called softly, "Missy, come look at this one. He's beautiful. Ooh!" The brown bare head of the young doctor gleamed in the bright sun. Something Ferguson said caused the leaning doctor to straighten up and throw his head back. His laughing mouth made chin and neck strong enough to fit his long arms and strong square shoulders. His face, wrinkled with laughter, hid his grey-blue eyes. "Oh, Missy, come heah!"

Jane came to the open, floor length window and out to the balcony edge. She responded, "Kian, you may need a man, but I can wait." She did, however, take a good look, and that may be the point at which she made the start of a long attachment.

Jane Herbert Wilkinson was the daughter of General William Wilkinson, brother of the noted James Wilkinson, United States Army. William fell at the battle of Fallen Timbers, and in a short while Jane was orphaned at the death of her mother. She had come to live with her sister, Barbara Calvitt, at Propinquity three years earlier. She was barely sixteen when she first looked on the back of James Long's head.

It was no problem, once she decided, to make his acquaintance. In a short while he resigned from Carroll's brigade, intending to settle in Natchez, while his detachment returned up the Natchez Trace. Barbara Calvitt, concerned with her young sister's infatuation with the doctor, asked her uncle, the retired General James Wilkinson, to speak to Long about postponing the marriage until Jane had reached her maturity.

Wilkinson, himself a graduate in medicine, found Long to be anxious not to lose Jane under any circumstance. Jane felt

CHAPTER FOUR

Old Hickory's shoulder wound had hardly drained since January 8, 1815. "Winning a war helps heal wounds," Long noted. He had helped his own group and British doctors, under a flag of truce, move the wounded from the field and prepare the dead for burial. Now it was time to move homeward, and see if the practice of medicine in peace was what he had hoped for. His orders were to proceed northward with a small squad of field corpsmen, twenty seven wounded Tennesseans and four wagons fitted as ambulances. He left with the good wishes of Dr. Hogg and a warm embrace from the General.

On the cold morning of February 10, 1815 Dr. Long brought the last of his wounded charges to a small guest cottage on the grounds of the plantation Propinquity, owned by Mrs. Barbara Calvitt. The plantation was between Natchez and Washington, Mississippi, almost on the grounds of Fort Dearborn, where the Carroll forces had rested before the long walk back up the Natchez Trace five years before.

"Peace" and "home" were the watchwords now. Long, still wearing his britches and boots, had traded his uniform jacket for a warm homespun woolen shirt. He examined a wound near that if married, she would be free of restraining family ties, and have a chance to build her own life with James Long.

They were wed at Propinquity on June 12, 1815, only six months after the victory at the Battle of New Orleans.[3] The wedding ball was the hit of the season at Melrose, people saying, "Jane Wilkinson is more beautiful than even Philip Nolan's bride, Cassie Lientot, ten years ago. Oh, I hope she does better than that lady. She had her baby but not until after that horse trader had lost his life in faraway Texas."

Becoming associated with Doctor William Cattlet, James soon attained his license to practice. This conferred the right to charge and collect for services rendered. Without the license, one could doctor but the patient could refuse to pay. His practice was successful, covering Natchez, Washington, and eventually, as they acquired land, northward to Port Gibson. Within a year, the young couple bought a plantation in Walnut Hills,[4] a hilly area above Natchez. James's brother, David, came down from Nashville to help with the extensive farm. Jane gave birth to Ann on November 24, 1816. The Longs gave thanks for the child, their youth, his success in practice, the booming farm, and all things.

In 1818, the Longs—James, Jane, Ann, and brother David— moved to Natchez. The trading stores the Longs opened up with W. W. Walker were growing: in Vicksburg, Natchez and as far away as Alexandria, Louisiana. Barbara Calvitt, Jane's sister, had recently moved to that settlement. Now James was more of a consultant, less of a practicing doctor. He went back to the old trading days of his boyhood in Nashville.

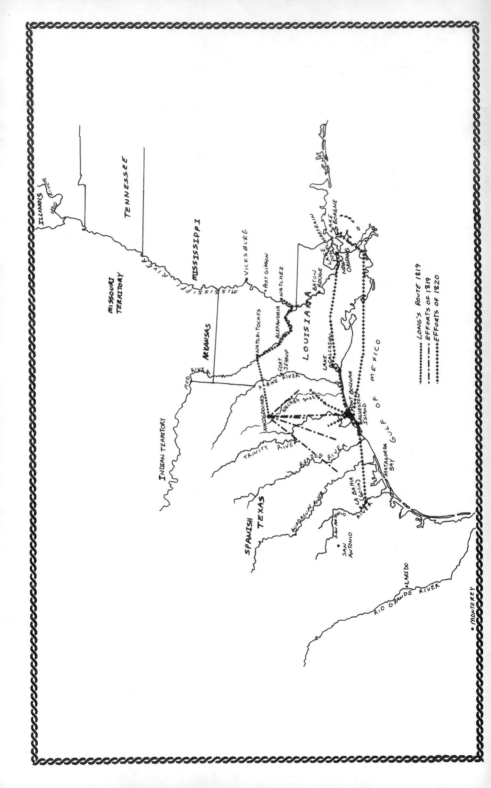

CHAPTER FIVE

At one time Spain and Portugal divided up the New World. Evidence of the division persists in the language of Brazil and in many countries in Central and South America. In Mexico for a long two centuries the country had writhed in resistance to Spanish rule. Spanish royalty, worn out by long efforts had finally quitted to Napoleon in Europe, and was increasingly unable to contend with Mexican uprisings or threats from Yankee supported intrusions. The Indian unrest, led by the priest Hidalgo, had put into motion an indigent cauldron. This was further fed by Jose Maria Morelos and his successors. Beginning in 1810, the Spanish Captain Peron Arredondo, at San Antonio, had himself succeeded in pushing out three Yankee settlers—Lallemond, Mira, and Gutierrez-Magee, the last at the Medina River in 1813.

Spain, anxious to hang on to her dwindling Empire, signed the Oni-Adams agreement in early 1819, defining the borders of Louisiana to end at the Sabine River. There were people like Moses Austin[5] and many others who protested loudly about the limits placed on American ventures. Austin said, "To give encouragement to a shiftless, sloppy power that has kept beautiful land away from good people anxious to turn its fallow state to homes and crops and happiness is wrong. The land

should be opened to immigrants." These sentiments were
shared not only by Americans, but many in a Europe trying to
settle down after the stirring Napoleon had given that part of
the world.

Ready to invade Spanish Texas were former soldiers who
had not worked back into the peaceful life. Hadn't they beat
the best of Europe, the conquerors of the great Napoleon, at
New Orleans? How long could the Spanish stand up to them if
they came to take the new land? Texas was less than a few
hundred miles away.

Dr. James Long, his brother David, and their partner, W. W.
Walker, were in the front row at a night meeting in Natchez on
May 12, 1819. Henry Foote stood on the steps of the courthouse in the flickering light of pine torches. He reported to the
crowd that, "one half million dollars has been pledged," to the
formation of a new army to go to East Texas. Horatio Bigelow,
a newspaperman, slightly inebriated, spoke of the plans. Volunteers would be paid, "in land and have chances to buy choice
land at 'way low' prices." The money so far raised was to buy
arms and a few cannon. "As soon as you get there and settled,
you can send for your wife or your girl." Seventy four of the
crowd signed up, sixty two of whom were veterans of the New
Orleans triumph.

It was announced that General John Adair of Kentucky was
coming to take charge, and lead the 'army' to Texas. The
rumble abated as one Hamlin Cook rose to state that John Adair
had other commitments, like running for Governor of Kentucky, and could not go. Henry Foote raised his voice. "We
are ready to go, we have the money. Seventy five men will be
three hundred before we get to Alexandria. We need a leader."

"We have one. If he will go, I'll follow him." This came from a young, husky one-armed man who stood on the right end of the front row. He ascended the courthouse steps near Foote, and speaking in a high pitched emotional voice, said, "him." He pointed to Doctor Long. "I knew him in New Orleans. I seen him with General Jackson and General Coffee and General Carroll. He can soldier, he can lead, and he even can take your arm off and save the rest. And he will."

Long blushed and raised both hands to silence the rumblings that seemed to become a cheer. They moved him up the steps. He couldn't find his voice to say, "No." He accepted, provided one more chance would be given to get Adair to lead. He promised to announce plans in two weeks. The crowd cheered and removed to nearby taverns, the more exuberant seeking the river road down "under the hill."

CHAPTER SIX

On July 17, 1819, Eli Harris, with a printing press and about twenty volunteers, took off for the Sabine River via Alexandria and Natchitoches. On the next day Long and a small group were stopped downriver for possible violations of neutrality laws. The Doctor returned to Natchez and got an attorney, who cleared him to proceed. Two weeks later he stopped to see his sister-in-law, Barbara Calvitt, in Alexandria. He told her of Jane, baby Ann, and the unborn, nearing term. As had been predicted, the infectious enthusiasm of these 'freebooters' attracted many restless ones. The invaders numbered three hundred, as they moved to Natchitoches. Here James and David Long, and partner Walker, arranged for supplies and money for the expedition. They moved across the Sabine River north of Fort Jessup, where a U. S. Army force was stationed to prevent the entrance of any American into Spanish Texas.

They entered a land held for more than two centuries without plans for use or development; a fertile land, heavily wooded, blessed with flowing rivers, and crying for settlers. Indian tribes moved through it hunting and, like the Spanish, little thought was given to settling or cultivating the soil. The seat of hemispheric Spanish Rule was at Havana, and power, such as it was, delegated to Vera Cruz, Mexico City, to Laredo, and finally to San Antonio de Bexar. From time to time a small ragged force would show up to enforce the decadent Spanish rule, but few knew what that was. One of the outposts of this feeble rule was at Nacogdoches, 100 miles west of the Sabine and 400 miles east of San Antonio.

An old stone house at Nacogdoches, a relic of religious missionaries, stood at the side of El Camino—a road leading from the Sabine River via San Antonio and Monterrey to Mexico City. This old house had seen several unsuccessful invaders, the last being a Latin-French-Irish group that put the flag of Gutierrez-Magee on a pole over the roof. As weak as the Spanish were, these invaders were put to flight in 1813. Two of them, Sam Davenport and Jose Gutierrez himself, were amongst Long's men.

Long arrived to join the early ones and promptly ran up the new Texas flag. Jane had made it herself—one white star on a blue field at the left corner of a red flag. A Council was elected. The young doctor, now called General Long, was elected President. On June 23, 1819, President Long declared Texas to be an independent republic, headed by a Supreme Council. In a long statement of purposes and resolves, "Texas under the Blessing of God is to be Free." Much of the document sounded like Jefferson. After Horace Bigelow got the news published, it was time to spread out and go to work.

A party under Thomas Johnson was to build a fort on the Trinity River and with that protection against the Spanish, and the Indians, if necessary, the men could then start to cultivate the land, build fences and houses. David Long led a small party to the falls of the Brazos river further south. William Walker erected a fort at a site that later became Washington (in 1837 it became the first capital of the Texas Republic.) Smaller forts

were erected at Pecan Point on the Red River, and at the
friendly Coochattie Indian village at the lower Trinity. These
were busy men. They were spread frightfully thin. Motivated
by owning large grants of beautiful land, they worked hard,
trading with Indians for stock, and the hope of settling down to
farming, family and peace. They looked back to Long at Nacogdoches for direction and supplies.

Long took a small group as far south as La Bahia in October
1819. A Spanish force there was subdued, but if that place as
well as the others was to be held, he needed help. Recruits were
trickling in across the Sabine. He needed more. A sea route,
a port of entry, was needed. He sent Bigelow and a small group
to recruit the help of Jean Lafitte, famed leader of the
Baratarians, at Galveston.

CHAPTER SEVEN

Jean Lafitte had gained a slippery suggestion of legitimacy in giving aid to Andrew Jackson in the Battle of
New Orleans. Under this guise he resumed piracy at sea,
which was his real and certifiable talent. Moving at will to raid
the Caribbean, he followed the ill-fated attempt of Mina to
invade Texas in 1813 by planting headquarters for his nefarious
ventures at Galveston Bay. He colonized Campeche, as he
named the place, with Baratarians, renegades all, men and
women. He built a fort on the mainland at Bolivar Point, with
a large main house, Maison Rouge, complete with a high
balustraded widow's walk and cannons mounted on the second-
story balcony. The tough colony was made up of pirates,
tradesmen, squaws, slaves and prostitutes from the alleys of
New Orleans. As the raids of Lafitte took ships as prizes, the
harbor filled with crafts of all sizes and purposes. When all
crews were in, there were more than a thousand people here in
1819.

Gambling, drinking, carousing and fighting was almost con-
tinuous, but one word from Lafitte stopped any internal trouble. The Caranchuan Indians were another matter. They
preferred to live on Galveston Island and to extend their mea-
ger luxuries by thieving from the pirates. The other side of this

irritation was the blackguards' appetite for female partners, and the hairless pubes of squaws were in demand. One raid ended in a firefight in which Lafitte used cannon to drive the Indians from the island. Captives were later sold as slaves in New Orleans markets; so much per pound of body weight. The Act of 1806 prohibiting the importation of slaves into the United States had made a new market for Lafitte.

A severe hurricane had hit the colony in the early fall of 1818. Lafitte rode it out at sea and on his return to Campeche he found it devastated. They worked tirelessly to restore the area, but the colony that received Bigelow in the late summer of 1819 was a fragment of its former bustle.

Long had sent the Bigelow party to seek aid. In the letter carried to the pirate, Long traded on his past acquaintance with Lafitte and in particular to the care he had given Dominick You, a Lieutenant of Lafitte. Bigelow had the opportunity to get drunk and offended the pirate, whose reply to Long was, "I await my brother, Pierre's, return. Then maybe we can put Governor Arrerondo (in San Antonio) away." In late October, word was out that Arrerondo was aroused, and that a force of Spanish under Colonel Paolo Perez was enroute to uproot the American invaders.

Long was desperate. A personal appeal to Lafitte was all he had left. He went to Galveston. They met in the Maison Rouge.

"Welcome, Doctor," Jean spoke with a silky voice. "We are honored. We are sorry that Dominick cannot join us."

"Thank you, Jean." The doctor was cool. "I am pleased to meet you, Pierre."

They sat down to a linen-covered table set with fine crystal, china, a heavy silver service, and linen napkins. The wine was dark and chilled. The doctor thought of being back at Melrose in Natchez. He noted a dark-eyed beautiful teenager who helped serve the meal of broiled fish in a Creole sauce. It was said that she was the daughter of Pierre, or the lover of Jean, or both. Whatever, she was an attraction.

"I have so little time, gentlemen." Long wanted to move the ceremonies to hard talk. He told them his forces had almost doubled. He outlined the extent of the dispersion of his forces. He told of the interdiction of supplies by the U. S. Army at Fort Jessup, making it difficult to support his men. He needed a port to bring recruits, supplies, arms and ammunition. Finally, Jean Lafitte accepted appointment as Governor of Galveston and was also commissioned a privateer. As he left, Long, shaking the hand of the tall, dark-eyed, athletic pirate, felt a sense of uneasiness. It had been too easy; it had come too cheaply.

As General Long left, Lafitte was writing to the Spanish overlord in Cuba. "I have just concluded a visit with a man from Texas, who tells me, in detail, of his plans to seize Texas from Spain. If you would give me five hundred armed regular troops, I will see that this effort, like the most recent threat, will not succeed."

Long was in a hurry to return to Nacogdoches for several reasons: 1) he had enjoyed but a short reunion with his bride;[6] 2) He had received a note from her that Alton Cook, who had come in to cover Long's absence to Galveston, was drinking and there was no discipline; 3) at the Coochattie Indian village on his way back, word came that the Spanish Colonel Perez had destroyed Walker's fort and routed his forces on the Brazos river. He met Jane at a spot called Josh's Bayou and sent her back over the Sabine to her sister and babies. On reaching Nacogdoches he found confusion, and but few remaining followers. He hid supplies and ammunition. He treated a straggler from Walker's routed command, cleaning and doctoring his wounds. He mounted the horse with the wounded one behind and, taking leave from the old Stone House, never returned to Nacogdoches. Word was passed for all survivors to convene at Bolivar Point, opposite Galveston. General Long gave his solemn oath to meet them there. What was next, if anything?

CHAPTER EIGHT

The doctor retreated, caught up with Jane and Mrs. William Walker, and escorted them to the Calvitt home at Alexandria. Here they visited the grave of tiny Rebecca, who had died without her adventurous parents' knowledge. Leaving Jane, he returned overland to Bolivar Point to the remains of his scattered force. He heard of the death of Johnson. On the upper reaches of the Trinity River, the superior numbers of Perez men spent three days in overcoming a stubborn David Long and his small bunch. Finally, surrounded and with a musket to his temple, David cried, "Fire and be damned." He was obliged. More than three hundred horses and mules meant for the colonists ended up in Spanish hands. The dejected men sat with their commander.

"Stay here, men. We are not defeated," James Long said. "I will come back by sea with supplies and more men and we will win. Repair the fort here. Spruce it up." He took off in a small pirogue for New Orleans.

After a few days of meeting the long, dour faces of old friends and supporters, he went up the Red River to see Jane and to hold little Ann. The few months since leaving Natchez and a peaceful life seemed like a century. His mind stayed on the need to get support for the men at Bolivar Point.

Checking his credit at Natchitoches, he found that what his dead brother David had escaped was financial ruin. The man they had left in charge, if not dishonest, was at the least inept. He even took a nighttime ambush shot at Long. The bullet lightly scraped the doctor's scalp. Long did not bother to pursue him as he knew the funds and supplies were nonexistent. He had to accept a gift horse and saddle to be able to return to Alexandria. There, he began to see the hope of potential financial support and together with funds from Natchez, he was able to return to Bolivar with supplies. This time he took Jane with him. The highlight of the return was a dinner with Lafitte on his last day at what he called Campeche. Jane accepted a dinner invitation at the Maison Rouge, since her reluctant husband was otherwise engaged with his followers.

Lafitte, by his piracy, scared off most of the Spanish shipping in the Caribbean. His hungry men made the error of setting upon an American Naval vessel. Under the Federal threat to shoot down the whole colony, the pirate gave up some of his officers for trial, and subsequent hanging, and agreed to get out of Galveston. Jean, an amorous soul, could not have found a more charming dinner companion than the 20-year old Belle of Natchez. She loved every romantic moment with the swarthy buccaneer, but rightly noted that all the pleasantries did not divulge what the man was thinking. Afterward, she shared with James the distrust of the man.

Lafitte departed Galveston, leaving General Long's small group the big house, now hurricane damaged, and scores of smaller structures. Bolivar Point fortifications were improved. The Longs returned to New Orleans, now more confident that recruits and funds could be found.

New Orleans, a town with a strong French flavor, still sheltered a few old Spanish Royalists. For years they had witnessed futile attempts to conquer Mexico. But Americans there sensed the decline of Spain in Mexico and the prospects of gaining new land was a temptation. Long sold them a story, "I've met the Spanish and we are stronger than ever in our fort at Galveston." He got support from Edward Livingston, who was not only a friend of Andrew Jackson but the attorney who represented the brothers Lafitte. Another important backer was Isaac Preston of the merchant firm of Bryant and Foster. This was high ground in New Orleans.

A new group of American recruits was lined up and two mature adventurers signed on as aides to Long—Benjamin Rush Milam[7] and John H. Austin. These two, accompanied by Jane Long, her daughter Ann, the slave girl Kian and a shipload of supplies, recruits, and settler families, sailed again for Galveston. Long, under suspicion by Federal authorities, went his route by land across Lake Calcasieu and Vermillion Bay, arriving about the same time as his wife.

The Supreme Council of Texas met again on June 20, 1820 at Bolivar Point. Of the original twenty councilors, eleven were there, including the old drinker Bigelow, and the great survivor Gutierrez. They reaffirmed their purpose. Reacting to agreements made in New Orleans aimed at giving new respectability to the expedition, they elected Edward W. Ripley, a prominent General and Jurist, President. Ripley accepted the post. An ill wife prevented his ever being in Texas. He carried out his duties by mail from New Orleans, while Long served as General in command of the Army. Long not only accepted, but welcomed the new arrangement.

At Bolivar Point, Long had a twofold purpose, to provide protection to the settlers who could then fan out to colonize the new land. The return on their investments depended on farming efforts; cotton, sugar, corn and food crops must be raised.

The second thrust came from many in the colony, who came for adventure; to defeat Spanish soldiers and to claim their rewards in acreage, not crops. The huge expanse of land before them had fewer than 5,000 souls living there, and but a few hundred tired and discouraged Spanish troops, who should be easy to defeat. If the two efforts could grow the Republic would expand and thrive.

In the summer of 1820 the cantankerous Caranchuan Indians reappeared on Galveston Island for a war dance. Long had expected this trouble, having learned from Lafitte of their offensive habits. He and Milam took a small force of soldiers across the bay and struck at the revellers. Surprised, the Indians fought back with fury, but finally were driven off by the tough Americans. Long's doctoring talents were displayed according to an account by one Doctor James Parnell, the self-designated 'Surgeon General of the Republican Army of Texas.'

> Two Americans were killed. A private Martin on the battleground, and a Captain Kimball Davis, who died afterward of wounds. Two lieutenants were shot, one in the leg, another in the hand. Five privates were injured. One had his liver pierced by an arrow; he stuck a handkerchief in the wound and he recovered. One bruised his spine, the third cut his foot on an oyster shell. A Mister Eddington was stung by a bee. S.G.R.A.T. Parnell himself got an arrow which stuck his cap to the back of his scalp. Commander-in-Chief Long used his broken sword to cut the arrow from the Medical Officer's head before he could return to his duties.

The Indians did not come again until after Long's departure, and during Jane Long's long and futile vigil in 1821-22.

Long kept his forces busy and saw the beginning of colonization spread into the land. Jane's presence lifted his spirits and had a soothing effect on the men and women of the growing colony. One historian said,

> Not the least reason for this was the tranquility Dr. Long achieved between soldiers and the civilian settlers. History has emphasized the commercial motivations of a crude filibuster, but this man had to have talent to inspire confidence, chivalry to attract admiration, generosity to give affection and firmness to enforce confidence. He was a man beloved, honored and obeyed.

CHAPTER NINE

In New Orleans, Ripley and his backers felt the tide turning to the Mexican leader, Agustin Iturbide, as the ultimate successor to Spanish rule. The planners moved to give Long's effort a more Mexican flavor. They moved old Gutierrez up to a Vice-Presidency and brought in a Mexican insurgent, Jose Felix Trespalacios, to be attached to Long's army. In a letter to Long, Ripley urged him to increase the planting of cotton.

> If you can select ground for plantations, a mer-
> chant in New Orleans can bring indentured Ger-
> mans and Dutch there for three years or longer, at
> $60.00 apiece. He has nine ships and can bring
> 3,000 persons a year. So spread out along the
> Trinity and San Jacinto rivers and we will grow.

He congratulated Long on the successful action against the Indians, but warned of warlike activities attracting the attention of "neutrality nuts."

Trespalacios arrived, a tall, sedate, well-mannered middle aged man. His purpose was to make the Republic of Texas effort more acceptable to the succeeding Mexican insurgency. Finding difficulty with his ideas about the value of a scrip he issued as currency, he returned to New Orleans, together with fifty colonists who wanted to be paid off and to move on to more exciting scenes. In early May, 1821 they had made an unsuccessful mutinous effort, and Long was glad to see them go.

In Trespalacios' absence, Long had to deal with a nephew of Trespalacios, Santiago Modelo. He had been given a commission in the army to assist his uncle. A woman in the colony, Mary Crow, using the freedom of speech guaranteed her together with the manners of a mother sow, had offended all the ladies and most of the men of the colony. When she came to Long's attention he admonished her to, "up your deportment." Using Modelo, who already saw Long as a man between his uncle and command of the Republican Army, she tried for revenge. Modelo became so offensive, Long placed him under arrest. Mary Crow was even more provocative and John Austin removed her to a house outside the limits of the fort. Modelo obtained a sword and a musket and headed for Long's quarters. He asked for permission to visit Mary Crow. Long refused. Modelo went out anyway, and as a file of men were forcefully leading him back, the group met General Long. Modelo moved toward Long, a knife in his hand. Long gave the order to fire, and Modelo was mortally wounded, dying a few hours later in spite of the attention of Long, and the other doctors.

Leaving the garrison under the command of Ben Milam, Long sailed for New Orleans. Here he found the discouraged Trespalacios, told him of Modelo's death, and with no help from the weeping Mexican, he got supplies, new recruits, and a larger ship ready for return to Galveston.

In midsummer a ship of the United States Navy put into port at Galveston. The Naval officers were impressed with the orderliness of the colony and in particular with the beauty of the young hostess, Mrs. Long. Part of her beauty was the flush of an early pregnancy. The friendly visit of the American warship scared off one of Long's supply ships, captained by Thomas Carroll. He took off for nearby Vermillion Bay, where a storm wrecked his vessel and the supplies were lost. The captain returned to encounter the displeasure of Long. He grabbed the ever available Mary Crow and the two left the garrison. They sailed up the San Jacinto river, settled, and raised a family, it is said. (Thus making not all of Texas of noble origin.)

Word came from Isaac Preston in New Orleans that Iturbide had gained control of Mexico. It was agreed that Trespalacios and Milam should sail to Vera Cruz and proceed to Mexico City if the rumor was true. They would plead the case for the Texas Republic's legitimacy to replace the Spanish at San Antonio. They departed September 1, 1821.

Three weeks later, leaving Jane, Ann and Kian in the company of the doctors Edgar and Allen, and a handful of soldiers to man the fort, Long moved out. He and fifty two armed men on a schooner and two sloops sailed to Matagorda Bay and up the Guadalupe River. Leaving the ships, they were joined by friendly Coochattie Indians and proceeded to a poorly manned fort at La Bahia (Goliad). The small Spanish force was subdued. The villagers seemed to welcome the Americans. Rumors were that Arredondo and his Spanish soldiers under Perez had switched allegiance to the new Mexican regime. On the third day, Perez showed up. After a hot fire fight, Perez called for Long's surrender. "We are fighting for the cause of General Iturbide," Perez announced. "Are you for the Loyalists?"

Long replied, "Of course not. We want Texas to be free."

Long and John Austin were given mounts to ride west to San Antonio. Laying down their arms, Long's men were deceived and taken prisoner. At San Antonio, Long and Austin were captured. In late October they were sent to a Royalist jail in Monterrey. Long wrote to his wife, sending her some money he borrowed from his captor, the generous Governor Guillermo Lopez of Monterrey.

Help, expected from Trespalacios, did not arrive. He was held temporarily in jail at Vera Cruz. Milam and John Christie were allowed to proceed to Mexico City where eventually they were able to get Iturbide to free Trespalacios. While Milam did not trust Trespalacios, they both worked to get General Long free to come to Mexico City.

In early February 1822, Long wrote to Iturbide from Monterrey.

> I have abandoned my family, my home, my
> friends, to serve this country of my adoption. I
> have contended for independence of Mexico for
> almost three years. I feel confident that the legis-
> lature will attend to my case and do me justice.

In early March 1822, he and John Austin met his friends, Christie and Milam, in Mexico City. The new Governor of Texas, Trespalacios, interceded for Long's release with the Emperor-to-be, Iturbide.[8] Long would not kowtow to this old associate to get justice. He wanted to plead his own case.

He was assigned comfortable quarters along with the many other foreign people who sought a hearing with Iturbide. Long was invited to have breakfast with a Colonel O'Reilly, who headed a delegation to Mexico from Chile.

On the morning March 22, 1822, he rose early. Ben Milam was in the room and was concerned for Long's restlessness. "Are you all right?"

"I don't feel like I am going to get anywhere with Iturbide. If anything happens to me, go get Jane and the babies. She has that new one by now. Be a brother to her, Ben."

He went into the area where O'Reilly was quartered, a part
of the Presidential Palace called The Inquisition. As he approached a gate, a young cadet on duty as a sentinel challenged
him. As Long reached into his pocket for his official papers,
the young soldier placed his musket on Long's chest, and fired.
In minutes James Long was dead.

There was official grief. A long cortege of forty coaches
led the body of Doctor Long to a grave in the non-Catholic
section of the cemetery near Chapultepec. In the minds of
Long's compatriots Milam, Austin and Christie it was difficult
to separate the chance or accidental fatal shot from a revengeful
plot on the part of the old man, Trespalacios. He had carried
bitterness against Long for his nephew's death, and may have
desired the removal of a rival bid for control of the new Texas
liberated from Spain.

James Long was a gallant man, self effacing, brave and of
high principles. He was a devoted husband and father. He was
a "young lion" to Andrew Jackson, a capable surgeon to Dominick You, a good boss to Ben Milam and a husband worth
waiting for at Bolivar Point through hell and a rough winter and
then almost forever by the "Mother of Texas."[9]

FOOTNOTES:

[1]Three days before the battle of New Orleans at the
Hartford Convention in Connecticut, Yankees had passed
resolutions insisting that Madison's administration cease its
war-like ways. "That there may be some compelling reason
for secession, or to allow each State to support an army, or
not." James Otis wrote this language to a beset Madison at
Washington in Gadsby Tavern. Otis learned of Jackson's
New Orleans victory, and returned to his Massachusetts
legislature to vote for a resolution to thank God for New
Orleans. In keeping with Yankee bias, Andrew Jackson's
name was not mentioned.

[2]Poindexter was later a Representative to Congress from
Mississippi. He had an opportunity to support President
Jackson in his fight on the National Bank, but refused. He
received a bill to indemnify the owner for the loss of the
little slave boy, but it is said he ignored the request.

[3]At a nearby plantation, Springfield, fourteen years
earlier, Andrew Jackson had married Rachel Donelson
Robards. The General asked Thomas Greene, who still lived
at Springfield, to send a young male black from their
quarters to the doctor and Mrs. Long as a wedding gift.

[4]When the Reverend Vick and his wife died at the same
time from yellow fever, leaving thirteen orphans, the Longs
bought their land on the river. It was on this land that the
town of Vicksburg rose.

[5]Moses Austin and his son, Stephen, during this time were organizing efforts to bring American colonists to Texas. In contrast to the armed efforts of Long and his predecessors, the Austins talked with first Spanish, then Mexican, authorities to make the immigration of Americans legal and unwarlike. Old Moses put a bad light on Long's effort to the authorities, saying that it was doomed to defeat. In the end, the Austins' effort was successful.

John Austin was not related to Moses Austin or his son, Stephen. He was a strong addition to Long's Galveston camp.

[6]Jane Long had given birth to her second daughter, Rebecca, ten days after Long left Natchez. With the aid of a gallant Natchez gentleman she, her maid Kian, baby Ann, and infant Rebecca traveled by wagon, boat and muleback through driving rainstorms to Alexandria, where Jane needed bed rest for two weeks. Leaving her babies with her sister, Barbara, accompanied by a few recruits, she traveled in short stages to Nacogdoches, reaching there in early September 1819. Quite a trip for this little mother, still under twenty.

[7]Benjamin Rush Milam had adventured all over the southwest, into South America, and was a connection between the Long Expedition and the conquest of Texas. He gave his life in 1835 in a successful attack on the Alamo. He was said to have sought Jane Long's hand in marriage after her return to Texas in the 1830s.

8Agustin Iturbide, an enterprising, bold, devious and cruel man worked his way through military positions in the service of the Spanish King, then left to join and eventually lead the Mexican insurgents. He waited but a little time to proclaim himself Emperor in 1822. In the face of rebellion he fled Mexico. In 1825 he returned and was promptly seized and executed.

[9]Jane Wilkinson Long was a true heroine, an able, loving and caring wife and mother; a kind companion and owner of Kian and a few other slaves; a brave and strong defender and traveler; a successful operator of businesses. She earned every right to her designation as the "Mother of Texas."

Sept 1821. Her husband departs on foray to La Bahia and San Antonio.

Dec 1821. Infant Mary Jarvis born at Bolivar Point, now deserted save for Jane, Ann and Kian. Very cold winter.

Feb 1822. Courier from the governor of Monterrey arrived at Bolivar Point with money and message from James Long, then a prisoner.

Aug 1822. A letter from Abel Terrell at Mexico City reached her and told of her husband's death.

Oct 1822. At San Antonio, where Trespalacios sought to help her get compensation for her husband's loss. Stayed in San Antonio area.

Aug 1823. Left by mule train, returning to her sister's house in Louisiana and Mississippi. In 1825 she saw Ben Milam, who brought letter and possessions of her dead husband. Four year old Mary Jarvis died in Mississippi.

Spring 1825. She moved with her sister's family to Texas, settling at San Felipe, the capital of Stephen Austin's colony. Here she opened her first boarding house. She had been given some land grants.

Spring 1830. She returned to Natchez and placed her daughter, Ann, in school.

Fall 1831. She returned to Brazos where the Calvitts had finally settled. Ably assisted by her alter ego, the slave Kian, she operated a boarding house here, paying off her debts, and acquiring property. She entertained Austin, Mirabeau Lamar, William Travis, and many other prominent Texans.

1847. She and Kian opened a new boarding house and hotel at Richmond. Kian died, leaving four children and several grandchildren. One of the latter, also named Kian, stayed with Jane until her death on December 30, 1880 at Richmond, Texas.

BIBLIOGRAPHY

Batson, Holly. *Personal Communication*. Nacogdoches, Texas: W. Steen Library, 1987.

Carver, Lois. "Benjamin Rush Milam." *Southwestern Historical Quarterly* (October 1934).

James, Marquis. *Andrew Jackson, The Border Captain*. New York: Bobbs, Merrill, 1938.

Lamar, Mirabeau. "Jane Long." *Bonaparte Lamar Papers I and II*, 1887.

Sapon, Lyle. *Lafitte the Pirate*. New York: Century Co., 1930.

Sowell, Andrew. *History of Fort Bend County, 1903*.

Turner, Martha A. *The Life and Times of James Long*. Texian Press, 1969.

Warren, Harris G. *The Sword was their Passport*. Louisiana State University Press, 1943.

_____

WASHINGTON IRVING'S
"GENERAL VON POOFENBERG"

James Wilkinson, M.D.
1757-1825

CHAPTER ONE

"It's a wonder this ink is not frozen too, Sir." Colonel Alexander Hamilton, warmed his writing hand, rubbing it briskly against his soiled white britches. He had just finished writing a letter dictated by his boss, General George Washington, to General Horatio Gates. It was to be carried to Philadelphia, post haste.

Washington had been angry, Hamilton noted, and rightly so. With the coldest weather ever anywhere (1777) and a "piece of meat not to be found near Valley Forge," it was a "damn poor time" for a so-called friend like Gates to be hooking up with that "cheating blusterer," Thomas Conway. The air had been blue, as well as cold, as the General vented his anger. It was one more reason that Hamilton longed for active duty to get away from his secretarial chores.

Thomas Conway, an Irishman who had served with the French Army, brought his self-admitted military talents to America. His offer to lead Continental troops had been accepted (the times were that difficult.) His stated enthusiasm for giving King George's troops a thrashing was welcome. Before long he expressed his belief that Washington might have been a good Indian fighter, but he was not fit to lead against Europe's trained soldiers.

Washington was not deaf. He heard the disturbing word that General Gates had received a letter from Conway and had not denounced the man. Hamilton, with his inborn sense of fairness, had tempered the blast to Gates, asking calmly for an explanation. "I've got enough trouble without this," Washington had fumed.

In September 1777, after a three month retreat under attack by Anthony Burgoyne's larger British Forces, the American Continental Army and its militia under the command of Horatio Gates, surprisingly forced the surrender of the British Army at Bemis Heights near Saratoga, New York. Coming as it did on the heels of Washington's great victories at Trenton and Princeton, it brought a tide of encouragement to the bedraggled Americans.

Gates ordered a young aide, Lt. Colonel James Wilkinson, age 20, to carry the good news to Samuel Adams and the Continental Congress assembled temporarily at York, Pennsylvania. On the evening of the second day of his ride, he dismounted to rest in a Reading tavern. There in the great room, at a table near the hearth, he was invited to raise a cup with Lord Sterling (James Alexander), a New Jersey patriot, and his aide, Major James Monroe. The confident, rash young soldier, probably feeling the flush of warm cider drinks, and certainly full of himself for his role in the Saratoga victory, regaled his compatriots with tales of the victory. Wilkinson was, at the moment, loyal to General Washington, his late boss, General St. Clair, and not so much to General Gates, whom he considered to be an indecisive old man. Wilkinson held that Benedict Arnold had "saved the hide of General Gates." Besides, as the grog loosened young Wilkinson's tongue, "That old man agrees with Conway that Washington should go back to his Virginia plantation."

When Lord Sterling passed these remarks on to Washington, the Conway Cabal came to a head, and heads rolled after the Court of Inquiry that followed. Conway left the pages of history. Gates was cleared but never regained Washington's respect. And James Wilkinson? It's of him, I tell this tale.

CHAPTER TWO

It wouldn't be fair to say that James Wilkinson, born at Hunting Creek, Maryland in 1757, into a planter's family, had the proverbial silver spoon in his mouth. But he had a caring family who gave him a good start in life. They were alert enough, for example, to take their lad to Baltimore at age seven to be vaccinated against smallpox[1]. Using family connections the fourteen-year old farm boy was sent for schooling in Philadelphia. This, America's largest city, was the seat of progress in the Colonies, owing to its location on the Delaware River, so close to the ocean and a safe harbor. It was the center of American culture, not the least influence coming from the Quaker people. Their devotion to industry, to caring for one another, their pride in public facilities and services, and their respect for private property, filled the city with fine stone and brick structures—homes, shops, offices, libraries and the most modern hospital of its time. Here the teenaged Wilkinson, bright, bold and inquisitive, began his study of medicine with the school's founder, James Bond. He read medicine, and attended the sick under the supervision of leaders in American medicine. He also made friends, courted charming girls and danced in the sedate but active society.

It was in 1774 that the first assembly, which was to become the Continental Congress, met in Carpenter's Hall, just across the street from the hospital where Wilkinson spent most of his days assisting physicians in the care of their patients, or at lectures on Materia Medica and demonstrations of procedures such as blood-letting and repair of fractures.

Wilkinson was not immune to the excitement caused by European soldiers—English, French and Dutch—with their spectacular uniforms. It was not long after the French and Indian wars, and military matters ranked high in the political life of the day. He confessed to Ann Biddle, the youngest and most beauteous daughter of a prominent merchant family, that he wished doctors were required to wear colorful uniforms so they would be more easily recognized and set apart as were the soldiers.

In the summer of 1775, having passed his tests, Dr. Wilkinson was licensed to practice medicine. At the request of his family (if not orders to repay obligations) he opened his office to practice in Monacacy, Maryland, thirty miles northwest of Georgetown. The times buzzed with tales of confrontations between English officers, and Americans. In the doctor's territory, a local militia met and outfitted themselves to train for combat. The doctor, not busy professionally, found it very agreeable to become a soldier and better an elected officer. With the brassy boldness that would shine in his life he took off to Boston, where the rhetoric and action seemed burning the hottest. Immediately he was made a lieutenant in militia and was assigned to a New Hampshire regiment under Colonel John Reed. At once, this handsome, intelligent youngster with the manners of a Maryland planter, bubbling with desire to advance his fortunes, was attached to the command of another American consumed by the fires for fame, Benedict Arnold.

His foray into Canada led Wilkinson and untried American
soldiers on a winter's campaign probably unequalled in hard-
ship in American history. In the winter of 1776 a letter from
the 19 year old Wilkinson to General Nathaniel Greene told of
the sorry condition of the troops under Arnold, a note that was
forwarded to General Washington and from the Commander-
in-Chief to the Congress. Quite a performance by a young man
who had hardly mastered the task of the morning shave!

He did not lead troops but became an aide to Arnold. He
was a handsome figure, an inch or so less than six feet tall, with
large brown eyes and a ruddy complexion. He sat a horse well,
in keeping with his upbringing on a Maryland farm. This skill
was a requirement for his duty to coordinate the units of command to meet the strategy of the day. Considering the enormous task before him, Benedict Arnold did well but short of
winning battles, and Wilkinson soldiered well enough to earn
his promotions.

The British effort, launched from and fed by way of Canada,
was designed to cut off New York State from Washington's
effort up the seacoast. Benedict Arnold failed to defeat the
British at Quebec but with badly outmanned forces, harassed
and slowed the British drive southward into New York. At the
height of this effort, Horatio Gates was assigned command of
New York. He lifted the young Wilkinson to a Major's commission, and brought him to his staff in Albany. In the late
summer of 1776, Wilkinson contracted typhoid fever, another
of the travails of the war. He found a place to rest and recover
at the New York home of a prominent New York family, the
Van Rensselaers.

Recovery came in three months, and Wilkinson reported for
duty with General Arthur St. Clair in New Jersey. It was at this
time the tides of war began to turn in America's favor. Wash-

ington, sore pressed, turned in the snow, crossed the Delaware River and badly defeated the British and their mercenaries, the Hessians, at Trenton. This, followed by the defeat of the British at Princeton gave the Continentals new hope, a lift in morale. In the action at Trenton, Wilkinson led troops admirably. He personally brought the news of victory to Washington's headquarters, and heard the General say, "a glorious day for our country."

Promoted to Lieutenant Colonel, he took leave to go on a recruiting mission to Maryland, and in Pennsylvania, where Ann Biddle was definitely a target of his free time. He must have attracted attention as he paraded in a colorful uniform of his own design—young, handsome, muscular, and not yet twenty one years old. He was a seasoned veteran and companion of famous leaders. In this city of 50,000 souls was the Congress, the civilian bosses of Generals. More important to Wilkinson was his old boss, Gates, who was recuperating from an illness that had kept him from participating in the victories at Trenton and Princeton. It just so happened that, as Gates got well, the Congress named him to the command of the Northern Department, where he had been before his illness. He ordered Wilkinson to his staff, and the young man, thinking he would get his General rank more quickly with Gates than by staying in the regular line under St. Clair, accepted the duty to return to Albany.

The victory that came at Saratoga in the fall of 1777 stopped the British troops, who were cutting off Washington's support from the west. It came after a number of battles in which Wilkinson was actively engaged. He developed a deep conviction that Gates was old and inept. To him, Wayne and Arnold won the field. Wilkinson was assigned duties to work out details for Burgoyne's surrender. It was then that Gates sent

him to carry the news of the victory to Samuel Adams, at the
Congress. On this assignment he met Lord Sterling and James
Monroe.

After a short bout of intestinal trouble, and having again
paid some social obligations, he returned to duty at Albany.
Washington's letter about Conway roused the anger of old
General Gates. He explained to Washington that some thief
had read his mail. He held that he did not support Conway. "A
big mistake has been made, all the work of a conniving under-
ling." This was too much for our young man. Not yet old
enough to vote, he was old enough to demand satisfaction. He
challenged the 55 year old General to a duel. "My honor
requires this action." The General declined. Wilkinson did not
know what the next step should be. Gates went to a Court of
Inquiry concerning the Conway Cabal where he was cleared of
charges of insubordination. In his defense he again accused
Wilkinson of ulterior motives in passing along lies about
Gates' relationship to Conway. This time Wilkinson, appear-
ing in person before Gates, got the duel arranged. They faced
each other, abiding by the codes of duelling, in the woods near
Albany. Gates' pistol misfired twice. Wilkinson fired harmlessly into the air, his young honor, he thought, unsullied.

The Congress appointed Gates to head up the new War
Board. Washington, having promoted Wilkinson to Brigadier-
General over the objections of many young officers on the
Chief's Staff, named him to serve as Gates' secretary on the
new Board. Gates refused to accept his late opponent at pistols.
Brigadier-General James Wilkinson resigned his coveted Gen-
eralship and went home to Philadelphia, a civilian doctor once
again.

CHAPTER THREE

I t had been about three and a half years since young Doctor Wilkinson left his not too busy practice to become a military man. In that short time, having barely reached his twenty second year, he had reached the rank of General, a fact that fit his ego well. He felt quite good about standing up to and defending his honor in the duel with old Gates. He was embarrassed having given General Washington some trouble with the Conway thing. He was sure that the American leader, and his staff, were relieved when they got a chance to retire this young 'busybody.' So, "if they don't want me to win the war, I have other things to do."

Wilkinson returned to Philadelphia, surveyed his chance to resume the practice of medicine and decided it was better in war time to join the Biddle family mercantile trade, then growing with the demands of war. Perhaps equal in importance to making a high station, Wilkinson courted, loved and won Ann Biddle to be his bride on November 12, 1778. Then followed work in the Biddle enterprises.

The war waxed and waned. Washington had discouraged the British in the Mid-Atlantic area and with the Canadian threat removed, the places for a winning solution radiated northward from Charleston, South Carolina. Howe and Cornwallis planned to move from the south. Wilkinson, as a civilian, missed the honors of rank, and when Washington, in a forgiving mood, asked him to return to duty, he was glad to get his old rank back. He took the part of Clothier-General with a Brigadier-General's rank, and the noncombatant duty to straighten out the mess of supply in the ragged Continental Army. Wilkinson enjoyed the travel and the contact with Army leaders occasioned by his task. Apparently he did his job efficiently, though Washington complained once that he spent too much time in his office in Philadelphia and on the dance floor.

A few months before the French fleet showed up at Yorktown in August 1781 and the surrender of Cornwallis there in October, Wilkinson resigned his job and commission and spent the next few years on a farm near Philadelphia. He was a member of Biddle's organization, a member of the Pennsylvania Assembly, and General in the State Militia, never out of the spotlight. He was a good family man. Ann rewarded him with his first son in late 1781.

By the beginning of 1783, all hostilities had ceased, and many soldiers, leaders and followers returning home found life tame. Tales of the spreading borders out of the old colonies, now States, excited men of ambition and Wilkinson was nothing if not that. He heard the talk of big untouched forests, rich land, flowing clean water. He couldn't stay in Maryland less than a decade before; he couldn't stay in Philadelphia with the prospect of new land, new power, new riches shown to him on the Ohio near what was to be Pittsburgh.

Land in large blocks was inexpensive and enticing. He bought large tracts down the Ohio as far as the Falls, where Louisville was to be built. He took Ann to Lexington, Kentucky where soon he had a mansion under construction, with a

formal garden much as the Biddles had in Philadelphia. He
opened a general store in Lexington as a branch of Biddle's.
As the role player he was, he was doctor, schoolmaster, merchant, politician and midwife. He stood by all activities there,
"not tall enough to be elegant but of good shape. He appears
strong and healthy. He has an open face, and is smart looking.
He speaks easily, is polite and gracious and cordial." And, as
his story from the start would tell, he got himself involved in
life on the frontier, far beyond the Lexington store.

In the mid 1780s life on the frontier was complicated by
signs of Indian unhappiness, fed by the British, who had not
renounced the western continent. In 1784, the Spanish who
held the vast Louisiana Territory began to look for expanded
trade up the Mississippi, and by their nature wondered if the
Indians needed any help to stem the westward movement of the
new and brash Americans. Wilkinson lived, thrived and
dreamed of more power based on his efforts in Kentucky, then
an extension of the State of Virginia. When the westerners
sought help to fend off Indian raids from the parent Virginia
they got none, and began to think of self-governing. Our man
liked the idea. Through a new friend and lawyer, Harry Innes,
Wilkinson came to know of the Spanish desire for trade, and
but little time passed before he had contracted with tobacco
growers and foresters to represent them in Spanish trade.

In the summer of 1787 Wilkinson rafted down the Mississippi, passing the Spanish blockade by the use of names of big
American politicians and generals. He wasn't faking; he knew
many. He met the Spanish Governor, Esteban Miro, in New
Orleans. They worked out plans for Wilkinson to sell tobacco,
honey, lumber and other produce. Miro would be exclusively
the buyer, Wilkinson the only seller, and no other suppliers
could pass the blockade. They agreed to split profits. As the

extremely good feelings grew, it would not have been past believing that Wilkinson might have sworn allegiance to the Spanish King.

Wilkinson, feeling his new importance, came back from New Orleans on a ship that called at ports in Belize, Cuba and North Carolina. He delivered Indian-made fabrics to his old chief, President Washington.

By February of 1788 he was back home, full of himself, his new friends and anxious to find his fortune in New Orleans. He enjoyed regaling Ann and the children with stories of his exciting journey. He lost no time in gathering goods to go down the river. In that year he shipped 200,000 barrels of tobacco, molasses and honey, a great deal lost to the hazardous river voyage and robbers on the way.

Wilkinson prospered. He enlisted an agent, Daniel Clark, in New Orleans to manage the trade. This monopoly lasted for about four years. Wilkinson returned to New Orleans. He lost no moment in expanding his knowledge of the vast Louisiana territory, including the tales of Philip Nolan's horse-trading in the far western Spanish lands beyond Texas. In the meantime, Kentucky had become a new state in the Union and our man sure-footedly worked Washington for favors on the frontier. That was what the gifts of Indian fabrics to the President were supposed to bring.

CHAPTER FOUR

By 1791 money was slackening off. Indian Wars became more annoying. Many tobacco shipments failed to get to New Orleans. Other politically able frontier people broke the Spanish barrier. Wilkinson was forced to sell some of his land. Some of his political opponents either envied or genuinely resented his lucrative setup with the Spanish, which together with his shortage of cash made him look for a new spot to develop.

He was offered a commission as a Lt. Colonel in the 2nd Infantry by President Washington, a favor from an old friend he could not refuse. He sold the store in Lexington and with Ann and the two boys they moved to a new bastion on the Ohio River, Fort Washington (later Cincinnati.)

Wilkinson served as second in command under General Charles Scott. He became a capable Indian fighter, leading units to destroy Indian villages, disperse raiding parties, and to assist in the building of forts in strategic locations where farmers could move their families close to military protection.[2]

By 1791 Wilkinson was made a Brigadier General in the regular army and began his service with an old friend from the Ticonderoga days, Anthony Wayne. Skirmishes with the Indians kept the troops busy and the construction of forts continued. The several years that passed were the best of all of Wilkinson's military service. Fort Washington was a great place for Ann to raise the boys—good food, clean surroundings, and an interesting social life, though limited to the military fort.

Wilkinson had a return of his intestinal illness. As he recovered, he reinforced his friendship with his New Orleans friends. The money, once flowing, now trickled in. He was able to do his military duties and juggle his far away interests, paid for in Spanish pesos, mostly by writing. In 1792 he held rank below only Wayne. Peace talks with Indian tribes held a promise that failed. It was only after a resounding defeat of the Indians at Fallen Timbers in 1794 that the grounds for peace were settled. In this encounter, Wilkinson lost his brother in combat. Wilkinson felt he had won the battle despite the incompetence of Anthony Wayne. Wilkinson brought formal charges against his old boss, not unlike the days with Gates and Arnold. Pursuing this, he went to Washington, but before he had a chance to 'strut his stuff' the old General Wayne died. James Wilkinson was now the ranking officer in the Army.

With the Indians quiet, with a new President, John Adams, in office, Wilkinson turned to the peaceful tasks of maintaining the forts and traveling from post to post. Ann, bereaved by the loss of their eldest son, John, began to suffer from respiratory troubles. In time they moved the family from Fort Washington to Pittsburgh with his new rank, and careful not to take chances with the distant and cold President Adams, he traveled over the country, making two trips into the Louisiana Territory, patching his relations with the new Spanish Governor, Carondelet, and finally accepting a home more suitable for the ailing Ann on the plantation Concordia at Natchez, Mississippi. Ann set up housekeeping here, the plantation prospering from the grow-

Ing Interest In cotton trade. Wilkinson continued his traveling
military duties to Georgia, Carolina, Virginia, New Jersey,
Pennsylvania, New York. When Jefferson succeeded Adams,
Wilkinson felt more at home. He stood by the new President
at his inauguration. He was the source of information to feed
Jefferson's great interest in the unexplored west. No one could
have told him more of the Louisiana Territory. He acquainted
the new President with the stories of Philip Nolan's[3] explora-
tions westward, and sent Nolan to Washington to tell the President first hand.

He made the acquaintance of Aaron Burr, who, coming a
close second to Thomas Jefferson for the top job, had settled
in as Vice President, the post for the runner-up in electoral
votes. Burr, closely committed by family ties to the school at
Princeton, saw that the two Wilkinson boys were accepted
there for their higher education.

During their time, Wilkinson got the duty to lay out and
construct roads to connect the various forts, wagon paths that
today carry the names of well-traveled highways. Among
them, for example, the road from Nashville to Natchez over
which much trade and some military marches were made, is the
Natchez Trace.

Treaties with the Indians, which had done much to encourage American settlements in the North and Central States, were
being extended southward as well. The stubborn resistance of
the Creeks to the loss of their land made for brittle agreements
during the years from 1796 to 1802. Wilkinson reckoned he
had traveled 16,000 miles and was away from Ann and his
family for more than two years. This was the price of fame to
this man, who seemed to love and honor his family.

Turmoil in Europe made each new day a time to assess
positions. Napoleon had risen, and the French had taken con-

trol of the Louisiana Territory through its conquest of Spain.
Wilkinson happened to be in New Orleans at the exchange of
ownership. He was able at this time to make an agreement to
become an advisor to the Spanish, who retained power over
East Florida.

In 1802 Napoleon, tied up in the conquest of Europe, disin-
clined to worry over Louisiana, was attracted by the offers to
buy made by the legate James Monroe. He sold the Louisiana
Territory to Thomas Jefferson's government for $25,000,000.
This made a new day for Wilkinson, all the talk and devious
plotting of the Spanish to expand power was now gone. It
could be an American thing. He must have been relieved to get
his loyalties straightened out. It was great to imagine that with
Spanish help you could head up your own nation. But, it was
perhaps better (and safer from the standpoint of a legal position) to work toward a place of power within the system and let
the old greedy dreams die away. With Jefferson's second term
in sight, Wilkinson plotted to be appointed Governor of the new
territory of Louisiana. In May 1804 he visited with Aaron
Burr, who did not run for reelection to Washington, but was in
contention for the office of Governor of New York. Burr
promised to urge Wilkinson's appointment to the Louisiana
position.

Burr lost the New York election. He felt deeply that Alexander Hamilton had been the main cause of that defeat and said
so. No amount of effort to calm the bitter feud prevailed, and
on a foggy July morning along the Hudson River at
Wiehawken, New Jersey, Aaron Burr fatally wounded Hamilton in a pistol duel, and began his painful descent into the
whirlpool of disgrace and shame.

Wilkinson became Governor of the Louisiana Territory with
his headquarters at St. Louis. He lost no time in sending out

exploring teams up the great rivers to the west. His own son led an expedition into Philip Nolan's old haunts. Perhaps the best known of Wilkinson's explorers was Zebulon Pike, whose long trip brought back the story of the fabulous west and led soon to Jefferson's own Lewis and Clark travels. These events speak well of our one-time doctor. But he wielded his new power in ways that offended too many people, and the duties were split—the military power was to stay in St. Louis and the civil authority to be headquartered in Natchez. Before Wilkinson left for Natchez, Aaron Burr visited him on the Mississippi and discussed with him the chance to move westward and establish a new life. In 1806 Wilkinson got a long letter from Burr, criticizing a new treaty with Spain that Wilkinson had just achieved. This was an agreement that the new eastern border of the southern United States would be at the Sabine River, dividing Louisiana from the Texas area held by Spain. The tone of Burr's letter seemed to implicate Wilkinson in treason. He saw a chance to be praised by his old Spanish friends, and more importantly to be seen by President Jefferson as a most loyal and dependable American. He sent Burr's letter to the President with comments that suggested that Burr was plotting to seize some parts of American territory and combine it into a new empire in Mexico.

Soon a price was on Burr's head. About this same time Wilkinson was grieving the loss of his beloved Ann to pulmonary tuberculosis. She died in the home of a trusted friend, Bernard deMarigny, in New Orleans. In less than a week, Wilkinson was called to Richmond where Burr was arraigned for a hearing. His trial was set to be held in Richmond in August 1807. Wilkinson was a prominent feature in this famous trial, being the principal accuser. On his side were the President, and many officers; opposed were people like John Randolph, the newly prominent Andrew Jackson, and many

others. John Randolph got under Wilkinson's skin with talk of
Wilkinson's deals with the Spanish. Characteristically, Wilkinson challenged the lawyer to a duel, and when Randolph
ignored the challenge Wilkinson published an ad in the paper
calling Randolph a coward. In general, the behavior of Wilkinson seemed to deserve the reporter, Washington Irving's char-
acterization of Burr's accuser as "General Von Poofenberg."
Burr was found not guilty of treason or misdemeanor.

Always protective of his public image, and self-assured of
his self-righteousness, Wilkinson demanded a Court of Inquiry
into the charges of his possible treasonable behavior.[4] In June
1808 he was found 'honorable.' He returned to Army inspec-
tion duties, not neglecting the ladies as he sought a replacement
for his lost Ann.

CHAPTER FIVE

The political implications attached to the trial of Burr dampened the ardor of Jefferson for Wilkinson's civil authority and he was restored to Army duty, with some loss of rank. In light of increasing trouble with England as Yankee seagoing trade increased, the new President, Madison, ordered Wilkinson to increase troop strength in the New Orleans area. It was a homecoming for Wilkinson. He met, fell in love with, and in 1809 married Celestine Trudeau, a cousin of Louisiana's Governor Claiborne. He made the terrible choice of locating his troops in a Louisiana swamp, and under severe criticism moved them, his new wife, and his headquarters back to dear old Natchez. But peace and quiet did not stay long—the bad choice of locating his troops tripped off the old questions of his loyalty, and again he faced a Court of Inquiry. Here, Roger Taney (later a noted Supreme Court Chief Justice in the Dred Scott Case) defended him successfully. At his trial he characterized his old New Orleans agent and now his accuser, Clark, "a witch," and an old Natchez companion, Elliot, as "a lover of washerwomen." Found not guilty he returned to duty at Natchez.

In June 1812, Madison declared war on England. One of his first moves was to have Wilkinson order Jackson and his Tennessee Militia to Natchez. On reaching there, Jackson was told he was not needed. On the march back up the Natchez Trace, Andy Jackson got the nickname "Old Hickory" for his toughness. He also got a very bad impression of Wilkinson, which he held forever.

In March 1813[5] Wilkinson was promoted to Major General and ordered to Sacketts Harbor, New York, to serve under Henry Dearborn. The return to cold weather brought on his commonly recurring intestinal complaints. Under his leadership the Americans were beaten at Sacketts Harbor, and a large American force was trounced by the British at Spears. In June 1814, Secretary of War Armstrong called for a retreat from French Mills, blaming Wilkinson, instead of Wade Hampton who had failed and then resigned. Wilkinson, now improved in health, had his chance to regain respect when he led a superior force against the British at Laballe Mills. He blew this chance, and was relieved of command in the 9th District.

After a short stay at Albany, Wilkinson returned to Washington, where he tried to reach President Madison. In his own words he described how he had tried to defend the capital city. The British burned it in July 1814. His old accuser, Armstrong, was fired. Wilkinson was without a job and he screamed for a Court of Inquiry to keep his self-esteem unspoiled. He began to put his memoirs into print. He wrote three volumes, 500 pages each, telling many tales of the War for Independence. He told all, pulling no punches.

His "memoirs" are a valuable accounting of the military contributions to American history. He was never bashful to tell a tale, nor sell a hogshead of tobacco, so he pumped out the pages. He was great with invective. Most of all, he pilloried the "timid Madison" largely because he would not return Wilkinson to his rank. He had a talent for the narrative. He got his final Court of Inquiry in Utica, New York, in 1815, with Henry Dearborn presiding. The charges were of drunkenness, lying, and incompetence. He was acquitted. His heavy self-dosing with laudanum to relieve his bowel complaints was held to be a part of his confusion. The trial was over; his honor restored. He wanted to be with Celestine, who had in the meantime lost her first child. His commission was not renewed. He had some income from the popular reception given his *Memoirs*.

CHAPTER SIX

In 1817 on a newly purchased plantation near Bay St. Louis, Mississippi, Celestine presented him, at age 60, with twin boys. Money being a constant problem he turned to the task of collecting what he felt were obligations due him for services rendered in earlier days, to efforts to make the Mexican Rebellion succeed. He had worked with Baltimore people in the forays of Mina and Herrera into Texas. He worked with an association of Americans and Creoles in New Orleans to further the rebellion. In 1819, with New Orleans associates, he had given aid to the young doctor James Long[6] in his attempt to colonize Texas. Wilkinson felt that he was entitled to recover at least 15% of the considerable sums that had been consumed in these efforts.

After five years of relative inactivity and with a wistful longing for someone's perception that he was still an important man, he decided to go to Mexico. There he would impress Agustin Iturbide, the new leader of Mexico, that Wilkinson was useful and worthy of being paid the money owed him. In a display of finery and carrying a Gilbert Stuart portrait of George Washington (the most revered American among Mexican Revolutionists) he called on Iturbide. He made a hit and soon was on the payroll playing the role as an unofficial Ambassador from the United States. In a short while, Iturbide became Emperor of Mexico. In his position of favor, Wilkinson was helpful to Stephen Austin and the first successful American colonization of Texas. He was able to help Joel Poinsett, also a doctor of medicine, in his duties as first official Ambassador to Mexico from the United States.

Wilkinson continued his efforts to get the *empresario* status in Texas which carried with it huge tracts of land to sell to settlers, but in vain. In 1824, he asked his son to sell some land and send him money. Around Christmas in 1825 he got Celestine to leave the young ones with friends and come to Mexico City. As the season closed the old doctor-general, worn out and feeble, again victim to his ubiquitous gut-disorder that had begun to trouble him in 1776, and caused his sorry performances in 1814, and was never far away, returned in fury. He wanted Celestine to take him back home He was justifiably weary and from her loving kisses his well warped spirit took leave from the old flesh on December 28, 1825.

CHAPTER SEVEN

This was an outgoing, self-aggrandizing man, accomplished and achieving from his start. He never for a moment lacked the nerve to energize his mental purposes. No American ever encountered nor sought out so many distinguished Americans as he. He begins with the famous Philadelphian physicians, his teachers: James Bond, William Shippen, Joseph Biddle, Benjamin Rush. He, forsaking his medical profession, came at once to the attention of General Nathanial Greene, and then Benedict Arnold, Philip Schuyler, Horatio Gates, Arthur St. Clair, William Van Rensselaer, George Washington, Alexander Hamilton, Henry Knox, Charles Lee, Tadeusz Kosciuszko, Henry Dearborn, Morgan Lewis, John Burgoyne, George Clinton, Gouverneur Morris, Samuel Adams, James Alexander (Lord Sterling), James Monroe, Henry Laurens, Anthony Wayne, Joseph Reid, John Brown (Kentucky), Esteban Miro, Philip Nolan, Thomas Jefferson, Roger Taney, William Henry Harrison, John Randolph, John Hamtramck, Aaron Burr, James McHenry, Alexander Von Humboldt, John Adair, Zebulon Pike, Winfield Scott, Andrew Jackson, John Marshall, Martin Van Buren, Agustin Iturbide, Stephen Austin, Joel Poinsett and probably a number I can't recall. Names like those to drop must have been a part of his charm, and enhanced his chances at bagging a big prize. This is a directory of early American history. Most of them were not only casual acquaintances. Some were so close that he challenged them to duels, or at least wanted to.

He gave short shrift to the potential satisfaction and comfort of being an honored physician. It is difficult to say when Doctor Wilkinson finally forgot all he ever knew or remembered about doctoring. All through his life, one form of colic or another (typhoid fever) betook him, most often when it was important that he be well. The favorite drug of the day for intestinal complaints, tincture of opium (laudanum) was his constant companion. In one of his several recorded failures, near Montreal in 1814, the charge of drunkenness was blamed on his overuse and the exhilaration bestowed by laudanum. He was exonerated. Actually, he was a moderate user of alcohol. He was also, in my opinion, a very lucky man, surviving three Courts of Inquiry in his time.

His training as a physician probably had nothing to do with his audacity nor his ability to rise in righteous anger as he defended himself and excoriated others with his tongue and pen. Among his outrageous machinations to aggrandize himself are found his participation in laudable creations—the chain of defensive forts in the north, and later the roads that improved travel and communication in the bustling republic. His curiosity and followup to explore the west and southwest gave impetus to the growth of America. And there is the probability that his exposure of Aaron Burr's plans may have spared the nation some bitter days and many lives.

In an unmarked grave in Mexico City lie the remains of this most unusual American. His soul has possibly inhabited the flesh and bones of other deviously adventurous Americans of later days, including no doubt, other doctors.

James Wilkinson, M.D., ambition never completely fulfilled, rest in peace.

FOOTNOTES:

[1]Smallpox was a withering plague in those days. The use
of cow pox inoculations to prevent the disease had come to
America only a few years before. At the time James
Wilkinson was vaccinated, Ben Franklin was still holding
out against its use. The weak showing of American troops in
Canada in 1775-76 was due in part to an outbreak of this
disease. During the bitter Valley Forge winter, Washington
got his troops vaccinated, a factor in the later New Jersey
victories.

[2]Military significance of names given forts established in
the midwest are familiar today—Hamilton, Jefferson, Knox,
Wayne, Dearborn. One such at Milledgeville, Georgia got
the name of our doctor, Fort Wilkinson.

[3]Philip Nolan, an Englishman, got his Americanization as
a young man in Wilkinson's Natchez home. Under the
influence of the General's directions he became an explorer
of land west of the Mississippi and into the deep southwest,
ostensibly to trade for Indian horses. His fabulous life is not
to be confused with the man of this name whom Edward
Everett Hale called a "man without a country." Hale once
had to explain why he chose a name for his fiction that
already had its own fables.

[4]As one reads the history of these times, Courts of
Inquiry about military behavior took up more of soldiers'
times than battles. In reading of James Wilkinson, time was
taken in Courts of Inquiry—for Gates, St. Clair, Dearborn,
Conway, Wayne and Winfield Scott, among others. It would

appear that this was a requirement to avoid being called a coward, a drunk or a thief. It must have complicated the art of war.

[5]One historian, commenting on Madison's relief of General Dearborn and sending Wilkinson to command troops in the East, commented, "Major-General Wilkinson, long-time Spanish spy with an appetite for booty and intrigue." General Winfield Scott, once suspended from the Army for maligning Wilkinson, considered Wilkinson an "unprincipled imbecile." John Randolph claimed that Wilkinson was, "the only man I ever knew who was from back to core a villain."

[6]James Long, a Mississippi doctor who married the young Jane Wilkinson, daughter of John Wilkinson, who had been killed at Fallen Timbers. Long's is the first story told in this book. Later, when Wilkinson was in Mexico serving at the pleasure of Iturbide he observed that the recently assassinated Long was "an imposter, dishonest, and slothful." This description of his nephew-in-law, killed by a Mexican soldier while in custody of Iturbide, suggests that there might have been a reward to Wilkinson for this obvious distortion.

BIBLIOGRAPHY

Ripley, J. R. *The Tarnished Warrior*. New York:
    Macmillan, 1938.

Mandell, S. H. and Minnegoode, M. *Aaron Burr*. New
    York: Putnam, 1925.

Shreve, R. D. *The Finished Scoundrel*. Indianapolis: Bobbs
    Merrill, 1935.

Wilkinson, James. *Memoirs of General Wilkinson*.
    Philadelphia: Small, 1816.

GENTEEL FILIBUSTER

William Walker, M.D.
1824 - 1860

CHAPTER ONE

If a movie were being cast, the character actor most fitting for the role of the leader of a platoon of American misfits off to seize the banana republic of Nicaragua would look like Popeye's Bluto, or John Matuszak, or Victor MacLagen or even an unshaven John Wayne. History must, however, be satisfied with what it got—a five foot two, eyes of steel gray, freckle-faced, one hundred twenty pound young American all-time loser—William Walker, M.D.

Let his only and younger sister, Alice Richardson, late of Louisville, Kentucky, tell you of him. This account was found with a bundle of other letters, tied in a fragment of Belgian lace, in a sewing basket where it had lain for more than a century, the latter fifty years in a Covington, Kentucky antique shop. The penmanship was precise, feminine and showed schooling in the ladies' academy of her home town, Nashville. In loving family remembrances she wrote:

November 13, 1860. I can't remember when I was first aware of my brother, William. I believe I was about four years old. It was in the kitchen of our big home in Nashville on a cold February morning. The big stove was glowing hot. Facey, our black servant, took some hot biscuits from the oven.

Somehow, that sweet black woman burned her hand; she
screamed and dropped the flat, iron sheet.

Sobbing aloud and very frightened, I ran from the kitchen
across the dog trot and into the big front room, then up the
stairs to mother's room. She sat up in her bed where she had
been lying. "Allie, my baby, what's wrong?" I remember now
how strong my brother seemed to me, sitting by mother's bed
with, as usual, 'Ivanhoe' in his hand. He had been reading to
her. He was about 12 years old, and his close-cut brown hair
seemed to make his eyes more gray, the grayest eyes I ever saw.
He rose, came toward me and, holding my face in his hands
said, "Allie, don't scare momma. Take my hand and we will
take care of Facey." He bandaged Facey's hand, cleaned up
the flustered kitchen, and everything was back to normal in our
house. That was William, always so strong and capable!

Two years later he went to Philadelphia to study medicine.
We missed him so much. Father had wanted William to be in
the family's insurance association or to become a Presbyterian
minister.[1] William was not a silly child like my brother James,
nor a wild one like Norvell. He could fight though, and had to
several times at school because some boys thought he was a
little sissy. I guess that was because he spent so much time with
our dear, invalid mother, reading to her, and waiting on her.
The first I remember of him was like that. That's why he wanted
to be a doctor. "So I can come home and get mother well," he
said.

I was about twelve when he came back home—in 1845 I
think. He had become a Doctor of Medicine at the University
of Pennsylvania in Philadelphia. Father was so proud he gave
William money to study in France, Germany and Scotland for
two more years. Back in Nashville, he was the best trained
surgeon in all of Tennessee. I was almost as big as he, but he

seemed much stronger. His voice was like music, his manners so European, and his searching gray eyes told you that he was a man, and that he knew his business.

In three months, mother's health became even worse, and in spite of all William tried to do for her, she died. William had come back to join Doctor Jennings in practice, but it seemed that mother's death made him an unhappy doctor. William had also spoken of his distaste for how doctors cared for patients in France. He told me that if he continued doctoring that things had to change. Mother's death changed him. He was going to leave medicine, turn to the study of law, and go away from home again. We all cried at dinner when he told us. Even father cried!

William wrote from New Orleans where he worked in a hospital and studied law at night. His letters were fun to read. He seemed enthusiastic and had much pleasure in speaking French again. Through a new friend, Mr. Randolph, he began to practice law. In a short while he decided to write for a new newspaper in the city, and to own a part of it. All of us at home began to plan to go see our 'big brother' and maybe get there at Mardi Gras time. We never got there. He was a kind, sweet brother.

We know now that he lost the girl he loved and planned to marry. Somehow, like mother's leaving, William was again changed.

We didn't see him again until he came to Louisville in the late summer of 1857. He stayed with Charles (her husband) and us for a few days. Oh, how he had changed. His hair was still brown, but much thinner; he was never fleshy, but now he was thin and nervous. His freckles had almost disappeared. It was as though he had consumption, but he did not cough. That hot, tropical country had tanned him and those once sweet and caring gray eyes burned under his brow. He was bitter about our own government forcing him to leave his job, not even half done, in that country. He said that he was going back.

William was kind and nice to us. I cried when he told me how James had died. We laughed a bit about Norvell, who was working then in Augusta, Georgia. The love we shared seemed little to him compared to the need he felt to finish his work in Nicaragua. I hated to see him leave again, so lost from us and our ways. The writing ended here.

CHAPTER TWO

The times have to be right for unforgettable characters to make their marks on history, very much the same, I reckon, that meteors don't just flash across the sky, but are expressions of certain forces at work (or maybe, play.)

While William Walker sought his training in medicine at home and abroad, and then turned to the law and journalism, America and Europe were not coasting nor standing still.

In the short span of thirty years (1780-1815) the upstart American States had bested England's forces twice, thus gaining stature for the new nation. Among the things America did not turn her back on was opportunity. While on a winning streak she passed and enforced, to a certain extent, the Monroe Doctrine which essentially said to European nations, "We will stay out of your yard" (where the French Revolution, Napoleon, and Metternich had caused Europe to boil like a hot pot) "and you, please, stay out of our half of the world with your expansionist plans." The turmoil in Europe divided and diverted the power of England, France and Spain from their otherwise certain-to-be dominant force in the Western Hemisphere.

In America, the peaceful settlement of the war with Mexico in 1848 brought back triumphant soldiers, many of whom would have preferred to be led to new chances for conquest. Some millions of square miles of new territory in Texas, New Mexico, California and Oregon were to be incorporated, settled, and brought into production. The apparent dissolution of Spanish power gave rise to native protests of colonial rule all over the Americas, and men like John Quitman, so recently a hero in Mexico, looked forward to leading newly discharged and still unemployed Mexican War veterans to take Cuba for the United States.

To meet these thrusts outward to domestic as well as foreign shores, there were, in the northeastern part of America, as usual, those who looked with alarm at the acquisitive appetites of the less-well endowed States. They called for peace, not conquest, and established neutrality laws. This raised the hackles of those who saw England making moves to control the narrow Central American Isthmus, where for certain there would soon be a Canal linking the Atlantic and Pacific Oceans, shortening the trade routes to the Orient. Already there had been moves to secure the United States' position in Central America. With the gold rush to California, thousands of the restless from America's east coast and from around the world moved in the direction of the California gold strikes. Entrepreneurs like Cornelius Vanderbilt lost no time in finding ships to take them to Central America for a quick trip to the Pacific. The alternatives were to go by wagon across the American west, either too hot or too cold for long oxen journeys, or risk life to uncertain winds and go 6,000 miles around the Horn. Vanderbilt's Accessory Transit System across Nicaragua afforded a short cut to the adventurers and cash to Yankee Capitalism.

Into these times and in the raucous, bustling town of intrigue and romance, New Orleans, William Walker came to seek his place. He was determined to make his mark. Short, slight and wiry, he was quiet and determined. His manners, polished by deliberate attention to his European training, had a suggestion of reticence. But the cold gray eyes spoke of the probability of easy offense, and a devotion to principle. His readings, in the quiet of his Nashville house, of Sir Walter Scott's Ivanhoe and Tennyson imbued him with gallantry and a need to defend the truth and the right as he saw it.

Here was a man in search of a cause. As it turned out, it wasn't medicine, nor law, nor journalism. It was death, perhaps achieved in the course of establishing America's "Manifest Destiny."

Read what his one, and perhaps only, true friend, Edmund Randolph,[2] mailed to Alice from his law office in San Francisco on September 4, 1860:

My Esteemed Lady and Friend:

Please accept my pitifully inadequate words which tell you of my love and sense of loss for your brother, William. Through the many years of our close friendship I have loved, nay admired and worshipped, his devotion to his friends and his beliefs.

Small and straight as an arrow he was. He came into my office on Poydras Street in New Orleans more than fifteen years ago, with a letter from Hugh Lea of Nashville. He looked like a school boy, suited in a tailored jacket and wearing a broad brimmed hat. Yet, his soft voice was manly and his manner reflected his European studies. We were at ease at once, and, as it was to be from the start, friends. He found comfortable rooms on Rampart Street and was immediately accepted to surgical duties on the staff of the Hotel Dieu. Each evening he read law in my office. He was such a pleasant companion and help to me, both socially and in the law, that my recollections of life in New Orleans are the most pleasant of times.

In little more than a year, William qualified for the bar examinations and was accepted with outstanding marks. I learned early that he was true, loyal and brave. New Orleans was a place of too many liberties, and little means to address offenses to honor. On an occasion I remember well, he served as my second in a duel of honor where I succeeded in settling a matter without getting wounded myself. The occasion to instruct your brother in the handling of firearms made me aware not only of his learning ability but of his sense of the advantage gained by being prepared. He became an excellent shot, but combat was not in his nature.

It was my pleasure to introduce a young lady from a fine New Orleans family, Ellen Galt Martin, to William. Their part in the social life of the Garden District caused in my friend a blossoming of good nature, quiet smiles, joyous if shy communications, and on rare occasions happy laughter. Their courtship was one of the rewards given me by New Orleans. She was a diminutive beauty, large brown eyes in a carved alabaster face, set about with rich curly dark brown hair. They were as if from fairyland on the ballroom floor.

*His practice of law growing apace still seemed slow to William. He was restless, and since Ellen had become a part of his life, impatient. Two friends of mine, desirous of publishing a newspaper reflecting their views, which differed somewhat from the other papers, (*Picayune *and the* Delta*) leaped at the suggestion that Dr. Walker become its editor. He and I purchased a quarter interest in the newspaper, the* Crescent*. Its successful start gave William the means to ask for Ellen's hand. In order to be able to do that, William had thrown himself completely into learning sign language. Only in this* *fashion could be tell Ellen of his intentions and corroborate his love. Ellen was a deaf mute. Mind you, Madam, that her beauty was heightened by her affliction.*

The newspaper flourished. Perhaps up in your area you have heard of Walt Whitman, the poet. In no small part his reporting for the <u>Crescent</u> *gave it an early boost. Your brother's stance editorially was different for the times and place, and attracted attentive readership. He stood for the gradual abolition of slavery, and for caution in the expansion of America into Cuba and Latin America. Of course, he was strong for the Monroe Doctrine and America's inherent goodness. He defended his stands in public meetings and became known as a fine orator. You will recall that he was honored to address his old school in Nashville in this time. He also had to settle a matter in the duelling oaks. True to his character, unwounded by his opponent's first shot, he discharged his pistol harmlessly.*

Early in the year 1849, I was entreated by my family to locate an office in California where new and exciting developments followed the rush for gold. When I parted with William it was more of a hurt than when I left my brother in Richmond many years before. William accepted the duty of closing my offices and he acquired my interest in the <u>Crescent</u>. *He would stay in New Orleans and marry Ellen Martin who, at that time, had only her mother to care for.*

It was more than a year later, a tragic year, that he came to San Francisco. In a broad-brimmed black hat, coarse woven heavy trousers, and a jacket more suited for travelling with a mule train, he greeted me solemnly. A foot short of my brow, tanned and toughened by exposure to the sun on his long wagon journey, he seemed fallen. His embrace was warm but he was not happy. In a moment he told how Asiatic Cholera came ashore with German immigrants and decimated New Orleans. Fortunately, Ellen and her mother, who had moved in with William, escaped the killing epidemic but, as New Orleans has experienced, over and over again, the dread Yellow Fever attacked the city and took Ellen away. "Once more," he said, "all I could learn of disease and the body did not give me the power to save her, or my mother." I wish I could have been there to sustain him in his grief. The newspaper, the practice of law, a former devotion to medicine—all of them counted for naught.

He came west to be a part of the outward reach for new lands, new ideas, new hopes. Through his sadness, I saw his strength, his talent, his will to achieve a future there only dimly seen.

To tell of San Francisco of ten years ago would be to relate a fantasy. William had come to a village with less than fifty houses built to survive more than a few months. The scores of tents and hovels were peopled by adventuresome souls, American, European, Asian, those displaced from Europe's struggles, soldiers not yet resettled after the Mexican war, and the footloose from everywhere. Hardworking miners, mostly losers in the gold fields, tinkers, tailors, farmers, greengrocers and many loose women came. The flow of intoxicating liquors, the exchange of gold dust from hand to hand, legal and otherwise, fanned the flames of raping and loot.

William had no difficulty in finding a place as editor of one of the several newspapers. He rushed headlong into the cause of law and order. Too soon, almost, I was called upon to defend him and his publisher from charges of contempt of court as he railed against lawlessness and corruption in the town, chiefly against the courts and the police themselves. He was jailed for contempt. This action attracted the attention of many good people who rallied. The citizens began to organize, and later were called Vigilantes, as they took the law into their own hands to administer justice, until the courts could overtake them in those duties.

As in New Orleans, William spoke his mind. He spoke strongly for the extension of America to new and oppressed areas. He was aware and much interested in the failed effort of two French adventurers to bring order to the Mexican State of Sonora, tucked up so close to the southern limits of California. In the summer of 1851 William raised a force in San Francisco to go to Sonora, and drive out the Apache Indians who were constantly raiding ranchers and miners there. He wanted to establish a separate State that might be later brought into the American Federation.

He had gone with 103 recruits, small arms, and the promise of continued support. His basis for payment to the men was in the form of land grants for service should a new country be established. In seven months, he had struggled back from a long and tortuous journey in the mostly desolate country, thoroughly defeated by the hard terrain and lack of support from his San Francisco backers. More than that, I had to defend him against charges of violation of neutrality by the Federal Government. The people of his area considered "Colonel Walker" a hero, and my task of defense was influenced favorably by this expressed will. I know you will be pleased to know of their opinion of your brother.

William chose to go to Marysville, a small town near here on his return. He practiced law there with my good friend, George Watkins. California was beginning to accept its status as a State given to it in 1850 shortly before William arrived. He succeeded in the law practice, and to my knowledge made his only attempt at party politics. He ran for, but was not elected to, a seat in the State Legislature from Marysville. Immediately, the Democrats, with whom he stood, assigned him duties to develop, define and publish policies. Acting as he always did, his stance pleased few in either party. Someone in Sacramento suggested that he be thrown from a third story window. It seemed he opposed slavery, but he was staunchly in favor of the agrarian position of Calhoun and Jefferson Davis, a position which might well have deserved some punishment. I mention this, dear lady, as it shows that William, for all his strengths, did not have a compromising bone in his body, and thus could have never been freely elected to any office in our land.

For several years he prospered in Marysville, and I saw him only when he made the trip to the city. His visits were always most pleasant and relaxing. On one trip he met William Cole, a young man from a prominent New Hampshire family, who came west to begin a newspaper. The result of William's meeting, and spending a weekend with this man was his return to the city and acceptance of the editorship of Cole's <u>Commercial Advertiser</u>.

Cole had just come from New York and Honduras where his family owned a large Mahogany plantation. Cole enthused over the beauty and richness of the unspoiled forests and countryside he had traversed. He took Vanderbilt's transit steamer across Lake Nicaragua. As Cole talked, your brother became engrossed. In the next weeks William had read every writing in California describing the history, people, geography and economy of that land. Cole had told how much needed were skilled people, investments, and the introduction of farming, mining and manufacturing skills into the land. With these a country like Nicaragua, which had seen six Presidents in fifteen years might find the stability of a government patterned after the United States.

The seed was sown. *Cole went back to Nicaragua, and got a formal request for at least 300 Americans who would come as settlers and help to establish a democracy. Concessions in land were to be granted to those who stayed. With this authorization your brother rapidly raised a company of fifty eight men and in June 1855 they sailed for a new land which had the aura of a paradise.*

Even though distance separated us, as did foreign borders, we corresponded regularly. William thought it was special that I might help him draft a new constitution for Nicaragua, since my grandfather was known to have influenced the American document. I went to Granada, Nicaragua in the fall of 1856 to see the constitution established, and to arrange for the transfer of the franchise of the Accessory Transit Company from Vanderbilt to a San Francisco group. I came down with a dreadful fever, and was forced to spend almost two months in Granada. Your brother's outstanding medical skill saw me through my malarial chills, and I returned to San Francisco, more certain than I had ever been that William had the correct formula for the improvement of Nicaragua and the whole area. Looking back, I can see that the changing of the franchise from Cornelius Vanderbilt to the Garrisons in San Francisco caused the withdrawal of any hope of the United States to give William the backing he needed to succeed. In that sense, dear lady, I feel a sense of guilt, just as now I feel I have not done enough to prevent a clash between my people and those who force us to secession.

There was an opportunity to help build a democracy in Nicaragua, erected on the shoulders of American settlers, whose muscles, hearts, and brains would be the foundation.

Under William Walker's leadership a generation of American culture would set an example for all the former Spanish colonies to follow. And bring to fruition the promises of paradise to the small countries in a confederation south of our border. Oh, the blindness of man, the unteachable human. When shall this day come?

William has gone, my dear Alice, and I have lost a large part of my treasure of friendship. I repeat for you what I said in San Francisco before William died, about those to whom we owe so much:

"You cannot tell today which pine sings the requiem of the pioneer. Some have fallen beneath their country's flag; and longings still unsatisfied have led some to renew their adventurous careers upon foreign soils. Combatting for strangers whose quarrels they espoused, they fell amid the jungles of the tropics and salted the rank soil there with right precious blood!

My heart in love.

Yours sincerely
Edmund Randolph

CHAPTER THREE

Waiting expectantly near Leon, Nicaragua for William Walker and his 58 Immortals was a dispirited rag-tag "army" under the leadership of the Democrat Francisco Castellon. Their being there was an expression of the political way of life for Central America.

The five States—Costa Rica, El Salvador, Nicaragua, Honduras and Guatemala—had declared their independence from Spain in 1821 and in 1824 established a Republic modeled after the United States. The fragile union, broken up in five years, then reestablished, and again unsettled by revolutions, abolished and finally expired in 1852.

Nicaragua had been in a constant state of revolution since 1830. The people (population 200,000) had never had a prolonged chance for self-government since the Spanish yoke was thrown off. Fifty percent were of mixed Spanish-Indian blood, thirty-five percent were pure Indian, ten percent white and a few were black, descendants of slaves.

Two parties contended for control, the Democrats and the Legitimists. They had contended so long that principles were hard to define, and the struggle was between the "ins" and "outs" for power. What is stated about one would just as easily describe the political state in any one of the five countries. It was expected that the "outs" would cross the border as refugees and remain to plot and achieve a "military" return. The party which won did not stop at a peaceful change, but extracted a price in lives and property from the losers. That much Spanish culture they had retained. In fifteen years Nicaragua had known six presidents.

After more than a century only a few plantations prospered in raising sugar, tobacco, indigo, fruit, cattle and forestry products. The beautiful land lay, to a large extent, untouched. The base for government services was hardly worth the loot that could be provided. Since 1849 the engine struggling to provide money was the Accessory Transit Company, put into operation by the cantankerous Commodore Vanderbilt.

The discovery of gold in late 1848 at Sutter's Mill in California, had attracted thousands the world over to that land; many took the journey across Nicaragua from Greytown on the Caribbean coast westward across the lake. But a fair number needed to return and so arrived at San Juan del Sur on the Pacific coast for the transit ride eastward.

Each passenger paid a commission to the Nicaraguan Government irrespective of the direction of his journey. In addition, the Transit Company was to pay ten percent of its profits for the franchise. In the course of the first three years more than 2,000 westbound tickets were sold at $500 apiece.

The hope at first, by Europeans, as well as Vanderbilt, was to build a canal across Nicaragua utilizing the huge lake for most of the journey. The United States Government had sufficient interest in such a venture to survey potential routes. The idea was given up for the transit. Steamships landing at Greytown on the Caribbean side, would disembark passengers and board them on small boats to ascend the San Juan River. At San Carlos on the eastern edge of the lake, they embarked on steamers that sailed across Lake Nicaragua to land at Virgin Bay. Here they loaded into horse-drawn carriages for a twelve mile ride to San Juan del Sur, the western terminus, where steamships sailed for California. Baggage was hauled in mule wagons. The whole caravan, sometimes of fifty vehicles, made an impressive parade. The drive through wild and exotic plants with its colorful foliage, the frequent torrential downpours, and the strange people, made exciting experiences for the transient strangers.

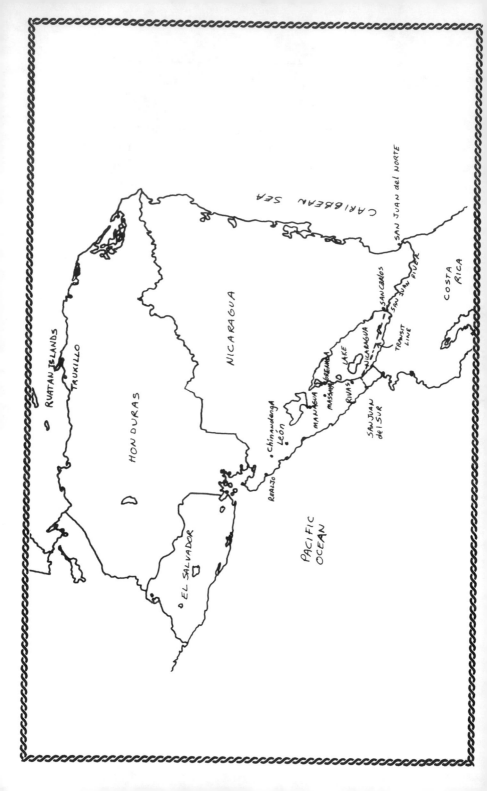

CHAPTER FOUR

In spite of the representation to Federal authorities on the sailing of the sloop *Vesta* from San Francisco, William Walker and his men were not going to farm, not right away at least.

His men, clothed in blue homespun, long-sleeved cotton shirts, armed with army rifles and Bowie knives, offered a contrast to the white-clad, loose-trousered Nicaraguan soldiers serving the Democratic forces. With little delay, Walker raised a native troop force of about 120 men and sailed southward, disembarking just north of San Juan del Sur. In unknown territory, in a drenching downpour, they moved to the town of Rivas and with boldness attacked the unwary Legitimists. Walker's men put up a good fight, guerrilla style, while most of the native force fled. Of the 58[3] men with Walker eight were killed, and twenty wounded. Disheartened, he retreated to the *Vesta* and returned to Leon. As he tended his wounded, he raged at the treachery of his new 'allies.' From that point on Walker took no stock in Nicaraguan promises.

In fact, the first pitiful foray seemed to steel him for his task. It would do no good to simply oust the Legitimist Chamorro and replace him with the wily and undependable Castellon. Better defeat the 'ins' and form a coalition in which the American held power. Within a month, made strong by a new Walker devotee, the native Jose Maria Valle and his 150 followers, and much encouraged by the 50 new volunteers from San Francisco with arms, Walker routed the Legitimists, led by a Honduran dissident, Santiago Guardiola (called the "Butcher" by Valle's men.) In fighting of less than two days, Walker's men boarded a Transit steamer, went directly to the capital city, Granada, and took control with hardly a shot being fired.

To the Americans, Granada was a Paris-like delight compared to the hustling and shabby environs of San Francisco Bay and the Nicaragua countryside. It was a small city of about 15,000 people, one hundred years old. The central plaza, lined with date palms, ended on the lakeside in the beautifully towered Cathedral. Many fine stucco homes rested behind bougainvillea-adorned walls. Shops lined the four streets of the square, their shutters rung down tightly against the expected rioting and looting that came inevitably and often with the change in ruling parties. Walker lost no time in settling into the alabaster white two-storied government house directly across the grassy plaza from the Cathedral. The Granadans, much to their surprise and pleasure, noted that the strangely clad, winning American forces and their white-clad darker-skinned native soldiers did not demonstrate victory in drunken behavior, armed robbery and cruel treatment of the unarmed and peaceful populace. Their small, dour leader had published the penalties for bad behavior and most who knew him knew also that he was a man of his word.

The American Ambassador, John Wheeler,[4] introduced Walker to prominent Granadans in ceremonies in the open plaza. Walker promised that Castellon would be coming from Leon and that it was his intention to form a new Government from both parties so that the peace that had come would be lasting.

Actually, the defeat of the Legitimist forces was not a feat to demand the attention of history. Certainly, a rag-tag battalion of untrained soldiers was not a world or regional threat. It was largely a routine clash between 'ins' and 'outs' that recurred convulsively throughout Central America.

Walker's call for the Legitimist General Porciano Corral to put away his arms and come to Granada as a part of the new Government was ignored for a brief time. When new reinforcements for Walker came by boat from the eastern terminus, San Juan del Norte, they met some resistance from Corral's backers and a fight broke out. Several transient passengers, including two ladies, were killed in the crossfire between the recruits on board ship and Corral's men on the shore. Walker held a military inquiry into the responsibility for the loss of civilian lives. The judgement was against Corral. A prominent Granadan, Mateo Mayorga, a former Legitimist and a man much beloved by Granadans was selected to pay for the crime. It dawned upon all Nicaraguans that this little gringo man, soft-spoken and very quiet, in his severe black suit and broad-brimmed hat was, underneath, a man of steel and vengeance. His own men were instructed not to brawl, or rape, or steal, and if they did, punishment was severe and quick. He meant what he said.

None of this was lost on General Corral. He promptly disarmed his men and came to Granada. He was appointed Secretary of War. Patricio Rivas was named President, thus disappointing Castellon. General Walker, as he was now called, remained in charge of the only armed people in the country. Almost as he had expected, Walker heard from his Nicaraguan friend, Valle, that Corral had hardly accepted his new title when he wrote a letter to Guardiola back in Honduras to, "come and let us get rid of this Yankee."

Corral could not deny his treachery. He was arrested and tried in a military tribunal. Guilty, he was given a death sentence by Walker. The outcry was great. The execution of Mayorga a few weeks before had been quietly resented. Corral had two beautiful daughters who personally pled with the "gray-eyed" one for their father's life, to no avail. Corral was publicly executed. Mourners soaked their handkerchiefs in his blood and, dried by the lake-borne breeze, these mementoes were hung in places to remind the people of the cruel, unforgiving little man from the north. Even Valle wondered whether he could get used to this man who led soldiers so well, and was so unconcerned for his own safety. Was he human? When Valle's troops had won in the past they could, "get drunk on aguardiente, have the company of women, and abuse and destroy the defeated enemy. Not so with Walker, not even to shove a man who but a little while before shot at you. Walker will never be understood by Nicaraguans."

Walker, the former journalist, moved rapidly to establish a newspaper, importing John Tabor as editor. He sent out notices of his intentions to the near neighbor countries, professing peace and predicting prosperity for his country and the region. He dispatched an Ambassador to Washington. The man he sent, Parker French, had many traits for an ambassador, many so bad that his assignment to this duty by Walker was mostly to move him from the air of Granada. None of the attempts to win friends succeeded. Many Legitimists from Nicaragua went a short distance, next door, for refuge with like-minded "outs" and there began moves to come back and put Walker out.

If peace was with Walker it was not of long enough duration to make the first transfer of land to his American recruits. With almost every steamship arrival at either end of the transit recruits came, and it was well that they did as Walker's need to fight for survival was constant. It was easy for Costa Rica, Honduras and El Salvador to raise forces to prevent the spread of the influence of the cold-blooded Walker. England, which had a deal to protect the Mosquito Indians on the Caribbean coast had no wish for Walker's success. They plotted with the neighbors to achieve Walker's demise. The United States, under international pressure to observe neutrality and with strong support from the northeastern States, were moved to enforce neutrality laws. They fed on the notion that Walker, from the South, would be extending the areas of slavery. In spite of a dominant force of politics against his advertisements in papers in California, the East and the South brought recruits on every ship passage. Moreover, on occasion a mercenary buccaneer, schooled in the arts of war, would join him. He had a small force and when it could be brought to bear, it was capable of defeating troops from neighboring lands, though they had four or five times his numbers. He acquired modern arms that gave him a big advantage over his enemies. He even had a one-man Navy under the command of Callender Fayssoux, which to the end fended off the frantic and futile efforts at sea from Costa Rica. The feeble input of the appointed President Rivas and various Legitimist and Democratic leaders, led Walker to call for a general election throughout the land in June 1857. William Walker was elected President in what may have later been called a Sandinista-type election.[5]

The Legitimist President, Chamorro, who met with Walker and his Immortals on his arrival, died in the outbreak of Asiatic cholera, which played a part in Walker's victorious drive to seize Granada. While it broke out severely in his opponent's forces, Walker's men were fortunately spared. Again the disease was a factor in early 1857 when, with but a few hundred soldiers, Walker and his best known soldier of fortune, Charles Henningsen, were able to snatch victory from the Costa Rican, Mora, and drive him from the country.

Walker's rise in Nicaragua is not a military conquest. It does not approach the feats of Cortez. It is an interval in history where a lone person, with a strong will and sense of direction, captured the reigns of a slovenly community and established local conditions to rule. The fact that the overall area and the community of nations didn't want it to happen would be force enough to cause the man and the effort to fail.

There was one more great cause, perhaps the critical one for Walker's star to flame out, and fall from the heights he had reached. The cause had a name, born in those times and still known in America, Cornelius Vanderbilt. Rising from his first humble start on a tug boat in New York City's harbor, he became a dominant figure in moving people and things in his native land. His prescience in securing a means to carry people back and forth to California over Nicaragua in his vessels was but one part of his entrepreneurial genius. When C. K. Garrison and Charles Morgan connived with Randolph and Walker to throw him out of control of the Transit, they asked for and got trouble. Horace Greeley said, "Walker sealed his doom when he took the franchise from Vanderbilt." The Commodore, as he was known, called in political chips not only in the United States, but England as well, to see that Dr. Walker would exit Central America.

In May 1857, a Commander Charles H Davis put ashore at San Juan del Sur, from the *USS St. Mary* with orders for Walker to surrender his forces, and agree to leave Nicaragua. Walker requested and received assurances that all Americans who wished to return to the United States could do so, and that all other officers and men of his Nicaraguan forces would lay down arms and receive the right to stay without punishment. This done, Walker boarded the U. S. vessel, was carried to Panama, and from there sailed back to New Orleans.

Thus ended the invasion of Nicaragua. Though the loss of American lives in Walker's filibuster exceeded those of the American Army in the Mexican War, the numbers are not staggering, as the conflict was confined to a small country. Henningsen reported that from the time of Walker's landing until his surrender, 2,518 recruits came via the Atlantic and Pacific ports. Of these, 1,000 died of disease or were killed; 700 deserted; 250 were discharged and the remainder surrendered. Against this small but well-armed and directed force the enemy raised almost 12,000 men in the neighboring countries. The superiority of weapons was clearly on Walker's side.

As the figures tell, a price was paid for the failed effort.

CHAPTER FIVE

The ultimate resource about William Walker's experience in Nicaragua is to be found in a work entitled *The War in Nicaragua*. It is told in third person style, precisely written, and according to competent historians an accurate account of those eventful few months. Its author was General William Walker himself. The purpose of the book was to raise funds and sympathy for his cause to return to the land that had elected him President, a fact that the people had not repudiated by another election since that time.

Walker had toured the eastern States for financial support. He had called on President James Buchanan in person, desperate for a reasonable explanation for America's intervention into Nicaraguan affairs and for hope of support for Walker's return. Every effort to recruit men, gather supplies, and outfit suitable shipping was frustrated by Custom and Naval authorities who concerned themselves as in the past with possible violations of neutrality laws.

In spite of this, Walker, a dozen of his old companions, and a company of recruits sailed for San Juan del Norte on November 14, 1859. They had a great plot to seize the transit steamers up the San Juan River and on the lake. With these they could mount an expedition that, by merging with friends in Granada, could repeat the conquest of a few short years ago. Walker's old cohort, Frank Anderson, showed up with the three captured steamers, just in time to find his leader arrested and in the hands of Commander Pauling of the United States Navy. Walker was charged with violating Neutrality Laws, and the invasion of a friendly nation. According to the records, William Walker was first seen to cry (at least as an adult). A United States Naval Officer was quoted as having said on that occasion, "General, I am sorry to see an officer of your ability employed in such a service. Nothing would give me more pleasure than to see you at the head of regular troops."

Walker was brought back by the Navy to New York. Here, in contrast to two years ago, an interest in his Nicaraguan enterprise was lacking. Even in the South where he had been a popular figure, it was difficult to raise funds or men. But the book raised some money and a small battery of his old fellow adventurers got aroused enough for one more try.

Morris Rudler, who had accompanied Walker in the ill-fated 1859 attempt at San Juan del Norte, was game for one more try, as were Tom Henry and about 40 young recruits. Rudler, most probably illiterate, was moved to write Alice Richardson, and she had bound his letter with the others resting in the sewing basket.

Augusta, Georgia
March 2, 1861

Dear Madam:

I asked my friend Louise Miller to write down for you about what your brother, William Walker, told me in Honduras. I reckon I was the last to see him.

I come home with him to Mobile when we was kicked out of Nicaragua in June 1857. He talked to President Buchanan and a bunch of Senators, trying to get us back to Nicaragua where he was still the President, but it didn't do no good. Two years ago we got a ship, and he and a bunch of us old friends went back and come near getting control of the Lake. But the United States Navy dragged us back out again. It was hard to talk anybody into trying again, because the young fellows who would go would want to be sure they got the land promised them and not just go and sweat and die in the jungle.

He wrote a book and got some money. More than that Tom Henry and Colonel Hornsby and Colonel von Natzmer and some others wanted to go again, because they heard that Honduras was in a mess with England, and maybe it would be easy to go that way and get back to Granada. We got a ship and sailed out of Mobile at night when the customs fellow wasn't looking. There was about forty of us.

We landed in a little old fort called Truxillo, and like we knew how to do, we sneaked up on their soldiers and took the town in about two hours. We needed to find a Honduran leader named Cabanas to get his help to get back to Nicaragua. Tom Henry knew him from old times. He went to the jungles looking for Cabanas' camp. He was gone about three days. When he come back, tired and dirty and thirsty, he stopped in a bar and had a drink or two. When he got back to the armory where we was based, he got in a squabble with a soldier that told him to stop smoking in the powder room. Tom had a terrible temper but the soldier had the gun and he shot Tom in the face. He was unconscious for five days, and we couldn't do nothing but to sit and wait for him to tell us about Cabanas, if he had found him.

Your brother, ma'am, took care of him better than a nurse could. He cut away the rotten flesh from Tom's face. He fed him, I bet, ten times a day, holding him like a baby. On the seventh day poor Tom wrote down where Cabanas was sup-

posed to be. I heard your brother say, "Oh, Tom! You came
with me from 'Frisco and I never saw you when you wasn't
wounded." He got out the little black doctor bag that he
always toted. He took a bottle of laudanum and poured the
whole thing into Tom's terrible infected mouth and down his
throat. Tom died that night, still sleeping. We went to the
wood hoping to find Cabanas. We hadn't got a day's walk
away when we was faced with about a hundred British sailors.
They was mad that we had taken money from the custom house
at Truxillo. They told Walker to surrender. He gave up.

The British took all but me and your brother to their ship.
They gave us to the Honduras Mayor and he sent word to the
Honduras President Guardiola asking him what to do with us.
In one week I was turned over to the British ship and was soon
on my way back to New Orleans.

Before I left the British ship I heard that your brother was
kept a prisoner for another week in the same room where Tom
Henry died. They took him to the edge of town near a wall
around a church on the beach; the soldiers lined up and shot
him dead, they said. They also said that two fathers took his
body and said prayers and buried him on the beach. I say that
because I know he believed in God and you would like to know
that he was not just thrown away.[6]

Madam, your brother knew no fear. Sometimes I thought he
was crazy the way he kept going back to that mixed up Nicaragua. But he was brave and kind to his friends and would never
let a man down. For that I miss him and send you my best
respects.

                                        Marius Rudler

CHAPTER SIX

Thus, by the crumbling mortar fallen from a native stone wall and but a few steps to the gentle surf of the Caribbean Sea, the shattered face and worn body of the little Doctor was covered with sand.

How had his short-lived career in medicine served him? Certainly it took a minor position in his life after the loss of Ellen Martin. Perhaps even before that, his move into an editorial seat, and the politics that then engulfed him, dampened any desire he may have had to return to healing. In the pitifully painful disaster in Sonora he had been the only surgical resource of his rag-tag invasion force. The need to amputate the leg and help heal his great friend, Charles Gilman, may speak of his retention of surgical technique. Gilman and his leader made a wooden peg which served Charles well enough to get him into position in an early skirmish in Nicaragua that ended his problems forever.

Asiatic cholera, which has the man-killing habit of leaving the Ganges periodically, was abroad in the world again in the time of Walker's conquest of Nicaragua. A few years earlier (1849) in New Orleans he had seen it wipe out one third of the population in that city. Accounts of that time spoke of unburied and abandoned dead filling the streets, and of the fright-

and people fleeing the city. Walker encountered cholera in Castellon's troops in his first forays from Realjo. He skillfully kept his "Immortals" away from the natives among whom the calamity spread rapidly. He does not record the reason for his men escaping the scourge, but it is likely that he made rules for eating and drinking, and for disposing of wastes. Once he had brought Ellen and her mother through the epidemic in New Orleans. Now he was able to limit the losses in his close followers in Nicaragua. Cholera killed Francisco Castellon, leader of the opposing Legitimists, giving Walker the chance to bring the Democrats and Legitimists together. Cholera again was his ally when shortly before his end in the late Spring of 1857, cholera broke out in the Costa Rican troops of Juan Mora. That worthy, in command of forces five times the number of Walker's, himself sick, fled. He implored Walker to be kind to the sick and wounded he had left behind in Nicaragua.

Walker took heart from the support he got from the disease, and, as he said, "from God!" who always gave help to the sick, wounded and prisoners in his care. He was not often praised for any of his activities but the press of America and Europe, on more than one occasion, spoke more kindly of this characteristic. As Valle had once complained of his lack of vengeance, most Nicaraguans were astounded and displeased with the softness he used on captured officers. Instead of stripping, robbing and disembowelling them, the order was to convert them to use in the cause of the new order.

His last moments with the badly wounded Thomas Henry in Trujillo underline the "doctor spirit" left in Walker. Henry personified the tragically misdirected loyalty that many of his men gave to this gray-eyed little man, once beaten to almost skin and bones in the desolation of Sonora, and obviously not a conquering hero. However, several of the Sonoran veterans jumped on the *Vesta* to go with their leader to Nicaragua. They saw his determination; they accepted his leadership largely because he was as good as his word, and he did not ask them to do anything he was not going to do himself. Intelligent men, some of remarkable talent, went again and again with him to the lost cause: Hornsby, Doubleday, Fayssoux, Swingle, Henningsen, Rudler, and others.

The loyalty given by his men might have been drawn from admiration for his courage. His frail structure had caused him to master his nerves. His sister mentioned his need to fight at his early schools. As was noted, he became a good fencer, and enjoyed the contests he was allowed to participate in at Heidelberg during his medical training years. Randolph taught him the handling of pistols, but did not need to encourage him to step into situations where honor required a reckoning. Walker fought three duels, one under the duelling oaks in a New Orleans park and two in the San Francisco Bay area. His first duel there with Graham Hicks attracted attention to the then-newsman Walker, for his cavalier refusal to shoot Hicks, who had twice shot at and twice missed, Walker. His last duel came after a quarrel with W. H. Carter. Walker did not fire at Carter but he suffered a Carter shot into his foot. He boarded the *Vesta* for Nicaragua limping from this unhealed wound.

He was hit by a ricocheting shot in the first raid at Rivas. Concern for his defeated men took his attention away from this minor wound. On other occasions he was noted for his seemingly cavalier attitude to gunfire. He suffered from a recurring fever, probably malaria, as most all who lived in mountains in Central America had the mosquito-borne parasite.

Bewildered, befuddled and belabored by the intrigues of the Spanish colonists and mestizo cunning, constantly watched and harassed by the British Navy on both coasts, and always the object of suspicion and charges of violations of neutrality laws by his former native land, he finally was brought down by the man, Cornelius Vanderbilt. The enraged robber-baron could not stand for the taking of "his" transit line.

Walker's experience as a lawyer helped him at times, especially as he joined his old friend, Edmund Randolph, in working for law and order on the Barbary Coast. The beginnings of the Vigilantes is rooted in their activities in those raunchy times in that City. He had a hand in that. No doubt his legal education led him through the confusions of the Neutrality Laws of the time. The force of Manifest Destiny pushed the limits of efforts all over the country, east and west, and certainly in the south. While his illness demanded he stay in Nicaragua, Randolph, with Walker, took satisfaction in helping to draft a constitution for the little state. Randolph was pleased to recall that his grandfather, John, had a hand in making the American one.

Walker's *War in Nicaragua* was published in Mobile in the last year of his life, 1860. He knew the value of the printed word. On his taking over in Granada, he set up *El Nicaraguense*, a weekly devoted to his version of world news, and local stories of progress in his endeavors. The book had the same objective as his paper, to attract support to his cause. Though most of his biographers, especially those of Latin persuasion, consider him a reckless, intruding Yankee, most give his book the distinction of being an accurate account of the action. It is written in the third person style and is very readable.

There was one other letter to Alice Richardson in the sewing basket found in Covington:

Baltimore Maryland
Nov 28, 1860

Dear Madam:

You don't know me. I served for some of the year of 1856 and some of '57 as orderly to your brother, General William Walker. He gave me a room in the Presidential Quarters. I helped him with the writing for the newspaper. I took care of the house using three women servants. I rode with him in the pretty woods along the big Lake. I went with him to fight battles at Masaya, Rivas, and San Jorge and if it hadn't been for him I would not be able to write this to you.

I went to Nicaragua from New Orleans with Colonel Fry in August 1856 and I was so disappointed. The newspaper ads told of the pretty land you could get free for going there. I was told I would get a hundred dollars every month and eighty acres of land in five years. When I got there, the Government was new and all we got was three blue cotton shirts, two pairs of blue cotton pants, brown boots and a black felt hat. We were given a pistol, a rifle, a Bowie knife and some bullets. Some of us went to the Rangers who had horses and mules. Some was foot soldiers under Colonel Hornsby, and others went to General Walker's Guards.

Since I couldn't turn around and go back home, I finally got in the Guards and for that I am glad. I got to know your brother was not just cheating us. He was working as hard as he could so that we could get out of the Army and go to farming like I wanted to do from the start. He wanted that to happen even more than we did.

Ma'am, your brother was really kind. He got up about sun-up every day and didn't blow out the reading lamp by his bed until about ten. His room was full of books, mostly about history and money and trade. The ladies of Granada, many of

*them very beautiful and of good manners, enjoyed dancing and
the company of men. Many of us were young and ready to find
a woman who knew the country and would help us when we got
our piece of land. The General was polite but very quiet among
the ladies. Our house had been the home of a pretty lady, Nina
Yrena, about twice the age of your brother. She had a lot of
men among her countrymen who admired her. I thought she
wanted to be the General's house-manager and maybe more.
He accepted her house, but made her live with her uncle on the
edge of Granada. I think he was smart.*

*We had only a few weeks of peace and quiet and good will
to make the city as nice as it could have been. Then came the
trouble with the people of the land. They took all they could
get from us and gave back only schemes for rebelling and
selling out to the Nicaraguans who had run away to El Salvador, Costa Rica, Honduras, and Guatemala. And we got no
help from the States, whose only real friend in that part of the
world was William Walker.*

*I listened to your brother as he told us the demands of the
United States that he give up the Presidency. He was sick, but
his eyes were clear and he spoke softly and sincerely. He
thanked us all for our bravery in defeating the enemies of
democracy in that land. He got promises that we would be
taken back home under the protection of the U. S. Navy. He
said he would return and complete his job. I got on a Navy ship
and came back to New Orleans.*

*I know now that my General was killed in Honduras and I
am sorry. He believed in God. Now he's gone and I am about
to go to war again, it looks like. People in Baltimore don't
know which way they will end up. I think America should stay
together, so I have joined the militia in Pennsylvania. I don't*

*want to lose again. I hope those nuts in South Carolina are
just fooling around.*

*I hope God gives you comfort for the loss of your brother
and my good boss.*

*Obediently
Sam Wickford*

William O. Scroggs, whose presentation of Walker is outstanding, had this to say:

*Even in his native city of Nashville, his fellow townsmen
believed his talents should have been employed to better advantage. In New Orleans, his repeated failures shook the faith
of those who once had believed in his destiny. In New York
"whatever harsh things have been said of General Walker, he
was at least no vulgar adventurer by birth, education, or habits, or the honorable purposes with which he set out in life.
Even those who deny him any claim to military skill or political
sagacity pay him the highest compliment to his moral force and
personal integrity." Another New York journal attributed
Walker's failure to win wealthy and influential citizens to his
cause. "He manifested a blind and foolish reliance on his own
destiny."*

*To Walker a splendid opportunity was given. A region that
for twenty years had been wasted by evil wars, whose heterog-
enous population had demonstrated its inability to govern,
certainly needed a new element to set it in order. Walker was
not big enough for the task. In six months he aroused against
him every force that should have been enlisted to his side.
Mastered by, rather than master of, his dreams, sadly lacking
in knowledge of human nature, overcoming resistance by insti-
tuting terror, wanting in tact and in diplomacy.*

To that summation might be added, he was unscrupulous,
uncompromising, and in the last days unintelligently blind.

FOOTNOTE·

[1]James and Mary Norvell Walker of Nashville, Tennessee, had four children, William, James, Alice, and Norvell. A cultured family, its servants freemen, its life was bound by Christian morals. It put much emphasis on education. William finished the College of Nashville at 14 years of age, having spent the last year assisting Dr. John Jennings as an apprentice. His study at the prestigious school of medicine, the University of Pennsylvania, foremost in the United States, ended with his Medical Degree when he was 19 years of age.

William's brother, James, left school to join his brother's adventure in Nicaragua. He was there but five weeks when he contracted cholera and died. Norvell, never a student, accompanied James to Nicaragua. His carousing with the American contingent caused his brother to reduce him from a captaincy to the ranks, and to extract a sentence in jail. Norvell never soldiered well, returned to the States, and recruited volunteers in Georgia for Nicaragua. He and his father survived the war between the States, and were thereafter lost to history.

[2]Edmund Randolph, born in Richmond, Virginia, was the son of a Virginia Governor and grandson of John Randolph of Revolutionary fame. He was admitted to the bar in New Orleans and served as Clerk of the Circuit Court there. He was an outstanding attorney with an impressive presence and probably a well-deserved reputation as a pistol shot which occasionally lessened a quarrelsome situation. As soon as his native Virginia seceded in 1861, this outstanding rebel California voice urged support for the Confederacy, but in that year he fell ill and died.

[3]Of the fifty eight (later called the Immortals or the Phalanx), a few officers had fought in the Mexican war. Three of his most reliable men and closest friends had been through hell with him in Sonora—Timothy Crocker, Achilles Kewin, and the man whose leg was taken off by Walker, Charles Gilman. There was a Doctor Alexander Jones signed on as Surgeon after a South Sea Island adventure had failed to disclose a treasure that he thought had been there. The men were mostly young, failed gold miners, unfortunates stranded in San Francisco, and pleased to have a new chance at adventure, land to be given them and maybe bronzed young females who might find a new face a source of excitement or maybe even pleasure.

[4]John Wheeler, a North Carolina politician, was Minister to Nicaragua from before Walker's landing and through his Presidency. He was a great scrapbook collector. Four of his twenty collections in the Library of Congress deal with Walker's career.

[5]Nevertheless, William Walker modestly accepted the honor and the position. A party held in the Government Building on this occasion found his American officers toasting their leader with imported wine (at other times not permitted) and calling him Uncle Billy (a term almost never heard aloud.) It is said that William Walker smiled!

[6]Written with a delicate female touch was the only marginal notationin the four documents int he basket. At the point noted was written, "Becoming a Roman didn't seem to help him." Could that be a Presbyterian lady's comment on Walker's late conversion to Catholicism?

BIBLIOGRAPHY

Greene, Lawrence. *The Filibuster.* Indianapolis, 1937.

Scroggs, William O. *Filibusters and Financiers.* New York: The Macmillan Co, 1916.

Squire, E. G. *Nicaragua.* New York, 1952.

Walker, William. *War in Nicaragua.* Mobile, 1860.

AN UNLIKELY RAIDER

Leander Starr Jameson
1853 - 1917

CHAPTER ONE

In the year 1867, in the Orange Free State in Southern Africa, a Dutch farmer calling on his neighbor near the Orange River eyed a queer stone in the midst of a marble game played by his host's children. This stone, shown to an itinerant Irish trader, finally got to Capetown where it was found to be a diamond worth about $1,500. Two years later the same Dutch farmer, Van Riekard, traded all the animals he owned to a native witch doctor for a large, brilliant stone that was judged to weigh 83 carats. It became known as the Star of Africa. Late that year, armed with hope and probably greed, many colonists prepared to dig, descended on the Orange and Vaal rivers.

Mining camps sprang up not unlike those on the earlier California and later Yukon gold rushes. Within a year, the camp at Barkely West had brick buildings. The river diggings were not fully developed when diamonds were found in the open veldt in 1870 on Dutoit's farm twenty miles from the rivers. The great find here became the Kimberley mines.

In the year after Kimberley came to life (1871) a sickly 17-year old boy, Cecil Rhodes, left London to join his brother, Herbert, on a farm in Natal. The purpose of his visit was to find a climate more suitable for his persistent difficulty in breathing. They purchased a farm and raised cotton. In the second year by the dint of hard work and using a new idea in planting they had a bumper crop. Herbert took off for the new bonanza land in Kimberley seeking a place to invest their new riches. Later in 1873 Cecil drove a wagon on the almost 500-mile journey to Kimberley, traversing a land so beautiful that its impression never again left his mind. Herbert returned to farm in Natal, but the delicate, gangling Cecil Rhodes stayed to direct his Kaffirs to dig for diamonds on their claim.

Kimberley was a jumble of mining tents and shacks clustered around four enormous holes in the ground. The mines were known as Clesberg Kopje, DeBeers, Bultfontein and Dutoitspan. They were "enough to make you nervous if you leaned over and looked down." There were scores of dusty miners bearing rawhide leather bags which were lowered and raised by donkey engines operated by white men. On reaching the top, blue colored clay, most often dry and dusty, would be spread out before the owner, who would have the clay broken up. Greasy white crystals, the object of the effort, would be eagerly sought and separated. At various levels in the hole, steps and stairs, walls, ramps, terraces and parapets, swarmed gangs of black Kaffirs, singing, humming and shouting. Their hoes and pick axes piled up great masses that were shoveled into bags to be raised to the recovery area.

The heavy physical demands of this mining created a demand for cheap labor. Blacks came from Kaffira, Zululand, Swaziland, the East Coast, the northern wilds of Transvaal, the Zambesi River and beyond. Eagerly they signed to short term work contracts. They reveled in the chance to earn money to buy arms and return to the tribe where they would be given an elevated status in the hunting society. The blacks came to work to save, buy arms and leave; the miners and their buddies in play and support came to earn, save, buy land, and stay. The almost nineteen year old Rhodes directed his Zulu workers to dig. They dragged out the jewel laden earth with mules. They dug, he broke up the clods, and claimed the valued crystals. Cecil toiled alongside Yank and Aussie. He dealt with German and Dutch speculators. He traded with keen dark-eyed Jewish diamond buyers who lost no time in getting to the site of the new treasures. He lived in a tent with five other owners. His companions in the new hotels and bars which flew the colors—Stars and Stripes, Union Jack, or Prussian Eagle—were traders, lawyers, gamblers, ex-officers of the British Army and Navy, younger sons of good families who had not found their slots in life, or who had already been kicked out of the nest. Money flowed like water from the riches of the veldt. Prices of food, tools, all commodities and personal services were high. Girls also came to provide a supply of care and pleasure to meet the demands of Kimberley. It was a place revealed in its kind of crude labor, varying successes, in its numbing tragedies and in its great bravery.

Rhodes made many friends and much money. In two years he had a trusted partner, Charles Rudd, to whom he left the management of his burgeoning mining claims and business interest, while he enrolled at Oxford. Cecil said he had to have a college education to be able to do what needed to be done in Africa. While in and out of college he won over rival mine managers and in 1876 he put together the DeBeers monopoly. The rakish entrepreneur, Barney Donata, the last to join Rhodes said, "No one else in the world could have induced me to go into this partnership. Rhodes has an extraordinary ascendancy over men; he tied me up, as he has everybody. You can't resist him. You must be with him."

Rhodes was rich and well on his way to achieve his Oxford education, graduating in 1881. He was still afflicted with difficulty in breathing, and repeated lung congestion. When he returned from London on frequent occasions to look after his extensive holdings, he lived in Kimberley and was a patient of Sterling Prince.[1]

CHAPTER TWO

D
r. Prince was becoming overburdened by the increase in patients seeking his care in the booming Kimberley. His appeal for an associate to join him in the practice of medicine was posted on the notice board at the University Hospital in London. The offer appealed to a young surgeon, Doctor Jameson, and almost immediately he responded.

Leander Starr Jameson was born February 9, 1853 in Edinburgh, the last of 12 children, all boys but one. His father, a Scottish Attorney, never sure whether he would be the leading lawyer in Edinburgh, a playwright, or a newspaperman, finally tried the last, buying two small provincial papers in Sudbury, England. There he wrote heroic poetry, propagandistic plays and was in general an advocate of lost causes, unheralded in his endeavors. He died when his last son was fifteen. Leander was bequeathed a generous endowment of eloquence and intelligence, charming manners and no cash. His mother came from a family near the Scottish border and with the help of her father, a retired General, she saw her remaining children into well-educated positions. Leander, known affectionately as Lanner, finished his pre-college work at Hammersmith, near London. (This area had an old castle at Holloway turned into a prison, at which, later, Jameson would languish a while.)

As a youngster Leander, though short in stature, had a bubbly and enthusiastic nature. He was undaunted by his relative poverty. In letters to his many relatives, including aunts and uncles, he showed an abundant love for human contact.

In 1870, aided by a loan of 100 pounds from his oldest brother, Tom, a Naval Surgeon, Leander entered the University College to study medicine. He won a gold medal for studies in Materia Medica and a scholarship in Surgery. He became House Physician and finally Resident Medical Officer at the University Hospital. He received his doctorate from London University in 1877.

Eager, alert, decisive and well-trained, he attracted the notice of men who trained him. Had he stayed in practice in the London area, he was a good bet to become a famed surgeon.

He was restless, even impatient for success. He took a week off and traveled to Paris to visit his brother, Middleton (Midge) who was studying painting there. During the same year he accompanied a wealthy American alcoholic across the Atlantic and back. He seemed to be seeking something. Julian, a brother who had gone to South Africa to seek his fortune, sent Lanner an uncut diamond, an indication of the fortunes to be found in that land of treasures. Leander dreamed of finding the money that would allow him to study in the medical shrines at Vienna and give him a leg up the ladder in London practice. Besides, he ruminated, "I've got this cough, this moldy lung. Maybe living outside London's foggy clime, I would feel better." There is little good evidence that the cough represented a physical disorder.

At precisely this point Prince's letter came. There is much in Leander Jameson's story to indicate that money was not an important motivation in his life. But, for whatever reason, money, adventure, or his "moldy lung," he arrived in Kimberley in 1878 to join Dr. Prince.

CHAPTER THREE

The older Dr. Prince met his new partner in Kimberley, now almost ten years old and a bustling town of 40,000 souls, still clustered around the gaping mine holes. Even on first contact, the new doctor was witty and full of life. He was an alert medium sized man, with dark eyes, heavy eyebrows, a straight aquiline nose, with a brushy dark moustache above a generous smiling mouth. The first impression was soon followed by admiration for his energy and competence. In a short while Prince and his medical cohorts found not only pleasure in Jameson's company, his roaring sense of humor, and his outrageous pranks, but his competence. He was well trained, skillful, artful, and was within a year, one of three doctors posted to the city's hospital.

Jameson had great charm. His skill as a surgeon brought him attention. Accidents were common in the dangerous enterprise of mining and surgical procedures increased. His patients ranged from mine owners to the precious and needed miners and their native helpers. On the occasions when Rhodes came to Kimberley now, Dr. Prince had him see Jameson also for his difficulty in breathing. The contrast between the two men was remarkable. Leander was born six months before Cecil Rhodes's birth in London. Though the same age, Jame-

son got his education without interruption. While he was so
engaged, Rhodes was farming, mining and accumulating an
empire, and was a rich young man when he met "Dr. Jim." He
was taller by several inches than Jameson, a man with an
unusually large head with clear blue eyes and fair-haired. He
was very shy, earnest and appeared almost solemn. Committed
dutifully to his ideals, he seemed always in thought. He had a
jerky way of talking, trying to articulate a thought without
producing the words. He had an active though slowly evolving
sense of humor that often ended in high-pitched laughter of a
teenager. He met an outgoing, clever prankster of a man in
Jameson, and they hit it off at once.

Jameson's practice grew as did his fame. He traveled to the
bedside of President Brand of the Orange Free State and helped
the old man recover. He was said to have a touch of irony,
especially with ladies who enjoyed their fancied illnesses.
Kind and generous to the poor, he was seen to be cruel to
incompetents. Praise was not always due Jameson. He was
said to be, "contemptuously intolerant of adverse opinions."
For example, an outbreak of disease broke out in a labor camp
of blacks on their way to Kimberley. Half the doctors who
came to investigate said it was small pox. Jameson was in a
group of doctors who called it pemphigus. When opposed,
Jameson told an Edinburgh-trained physician, "Stuff and non-
sense, it shows how little you know." Jameson's position,
popular with mine owners, prevailed. He was wrong—the
smallpox outbreak caused 2,000 cases and 700 deaths before
vaccination stopped the scourge. Jameson was sued by the
doctor he offended, and he countersued, without either side
winning. Jameson's reputation and popularity were undimin-
ished.

His partner, Dr. Prince, got into a mess with a young woman patient whose irate husband found Prince at the private Kimberley Club, struck him in the face, and challenged him to a duel. After extended efforts to talk to the man, Dr. Prince went to court and was exonerated of the lady's charges. This drawn-out incident finished the enthusiasm of Prince to continue the practice of medicine. He retired to Durban in 1881.

In this year, Rhodes, a graduate of Oxford, was elected Assemblyman to the Cape Parliament from Berkeley West. He also took over as President of the Charter Company, the holding company of the mines, merchandising enterprises, and much land. The Company aimed to control lands in the Transvaal and north of that state. Rhodes had selected Neville Pickering, a young engineer and now constant companion of Rhodes, to be Secretary of the Company. Jameson took over sole responsibility for Rhodes's health, and socially spent much time with Rhodes and Pickering. The three often rode and hunted on the veldt, and spent relaxing moments enjoying conversations about the doings of their world. In 1884 Pickering was thrown from a horse and received internal injuries from which he never recovered. In 1886 Rhodes, returning from an extended visit to newly found gold mines on the Witwatersrand near Johannesburg, sat by the dying Pickering's side with Dr. Jameson until the end. After the young man's death, Rhodes moved into Jameson's corrugated tin roofed covered cottage with the wide verandahs, across the street from the very important Kimberley Club. This was a big step on the way to changing the doctor's lifestyle.

Rhodes had his Oxford degree. Now he concentrated on his dream and plan to consolidate British interests in Africa. He had the money, he was building his political bed. As he saw his work before him, the first task was to establish control of nearby Bechuanaland and the wild country north of the Transvaal.

The Matabele tribes had broken away from the Zulus after their disrupting defeat by the Boers in 1867. In the times of the earlier great trek, Zulus had swarmed over the Free State and Transvaal. Defeated, the Matabeles were led into lands north and east of Bechuanaland where they easily reduced the Mashona and lesser tribes to a servile status. In 1868, Lobengula succeeded his warrior father as Chief of the Matabeles. They lived a life organized for battle. Their young men, raised on beef, a diet that killed the weak with dysentery, made the survivors strong. They were trained to fight. No youth in this order could marry until he had been bloodied in a fight and was thirty-five years of age. Almost yearly there were raids on the Mashona and other tribes for cattle and women. These attacks were preceded by impressive war dances, soldiers of the various regiments garbed in gorgeous and often terrifying trappings. These frantic doings always ended in feasts before the raids. After the defeat of the Zulus, the Matabeles were the most fiercely formidable of blacks in South Africa. By staying north of the Transvaal, they avoided the Boers. They made friends with hunters and traders who ventured into their bounds.

Ten years before, Rhodes and his brother, Herbert, had made an ox-cart exploration into this territory, and as was typical, Cecil bought a tract of land there. Already miners had found some gold north of Transvaal in the Tati area. The gold find brought the acquisitive and with them nationalistic interests. Chief Lobengula was surrounded by agents of many different nations—Boer, English, French, Portugeuse, German, Dutch—all wanting concessions. These offers gave the chief the choice of the world, it seemed. Paul Kruger of the Transvaal appeared to have the inside track. Rhodes selected the son of a famed missionary as his agent to hold off the Boer's offer until he could get his partner, Charles Rudd, to personally persuade Lobengula that Rhodes could give him the most. Rudd got there and with the promise to give what native tribesmen wanted the most—1,000 rifles and ammunition, and what the Chief wanted most—a steamer on the Zambesi River just like Stanley's, Rhodes got the concession.

Concessions like this required the approval of Queen Victoria. As they waited a prolonged time for this, Lobengula gave in to the old pressures that had not disappeared. Before Rhodes would go to London to hurry the approval, he wanted to ask his cottage mate a favor. Would he go to Lobengula and hold the Charter Company's rights?

Dr. Jim had played the role of the man about town for more than ten years. His practice was lucrative and professionally he was held in the highest regard. Socially, his matched pair of spirited black horses racing him around the town gave the impression of a bold, reckless man. At the Kimberley Club he was known to gamble successfully at poker. It was said that while others used alcoholic drink to fortify their judgments, he preferred ginger ale. The local saying for his bold behavior was, "he's gone to the Shebeens, where the 'dop' flowed freely and dancing girls were auctioned off." The doctor never settled for one lady, though he was not insensitive to their charms.

He did not keep his accounts well, which seemed to fit with his daring as a gambler. He gave the appearance of not being a reader, but in private he was a rabid fan of Sir Walter Scott and Alfred Tennyson. Under his nonchalant and almost cynical manner, ambition coiled, ready for a chance to be released. At age 36 he was about 5 foot, 9 inches tall, and weighed 150 pounds of solid flesh. He kept fit by frequent hunts on the veldt with a new friend and fellow physician, Rutherford Harris. Unsuccessful in practice, Harris was a skilled hunter, Jameson's tutor in the ways of forest and veldt.

The increasing demands of a growing practice seemed to stifle him. Life in Kimberley had settled down. The greatest excitement now came from the boom at the Johannesburg gold fields. The more sober Kimberley was banking and supplying the frantic gold miners on the Rand. While the showy people of Kimberley strutted at the club, Dr. Jim withdrew, preferring to join Cecil Rhodes and his "12 apostles" in their little tin-roofed bungalow. Here, the leader was the "practical vision-ary" Cecil Rhodes, surrounded by Charles Rudd, a miner, and his first partner; Oxford buddies Rockfort Maguire and Charles Metcalf; South Africa's best money manager, the Hamburger Albert Beit; Rutherford Harris; and finally, but above all in Rhodes' mind, was his roommate, the caring Leander Jameson. More and more he felt drawn to Rhodes.

A scene in the cottage might have been:

Rhodes, rolling deep into an overstuffed chair, jerkily re-peating brief statements, hunting words awkwardly to go with his grand and roaring ideas; Jameson lounging across from him, his feet up on a small table. As usual he is puffing a cigarette.

Rhodes is talking of the north country, the great plateau, a country meant for white men. It could be like America—home-steads, villages, cities, railways. As big as the United States, too. "We could put Africa together, just like we did the mines. An amalgamation, a Federation!"

And Jameson questions, "Where do you get the seaports? How to build the roads, the railroads?"

They argue; they agree.

Rhodes says, "Rudd did a great job. He is a good man. But when he left, Lobengula, the old king, floated in an awful vacuum with crooks and human snakes."

Jameson, feeling the direction this conversation is taking, says, "I'm sleepy, and I'm going to bed."

"But you are going, aren't you?"

"What about my practice? I can't just walk away."

"You're coming back. You won't lose a patient."

The doctor gave up his practice to a partner, and agreed to go to the Matabeleland. He was now working for his hero, Cecil Rhodes, a man (ask Barney Banato) not easy to deny.

CHAPTER FOUR

The journey of the two doctors, Jameson and Harris, to King Lobengula's main camp (kraal) at Bulawago took several weeks. On arrival, as Rhodes had feared, they found the black chief, surrounded by adventuresome pests confusing the King with enticing offers for rights to hunt, mine or trade.

The huge old man sat in agony on an old condensed milk packing case. He towered above six feet, and weighed three hundred pounds. He had glossy black skin stretched over a broad and deep chest. His nakedness, complete except for a blue Kaffir loin cloth and a Zulu headdress, emphasized his great strength. Around him in clusters were his sixty wives, separated by about half that number of sycophants murmuring the equivalent of, "You are the greatest."

But the majestic figure was sad and sick, and therein lay the chance for Dr. Jim's success. Lobengula was almost blinded with conjunctivitis aggravated by a witch doctor's concoction. Jameson, the diagnostician, saw that the King's aching was due in a large part to gout. The judicious use of morphine brought quick relief and like so many of Jameson's patients, Lobengula became his grateful friend. Moreover, careful washing of the Chief's infected eyes restored his sight. In the ten-day visit,

Rhodes' Company had the desired concessions, the doctors were feasted, and the King, as good as new, had his arms and coveted 'Stanley-type steamboat.'

This trip convinced Rhodes that Dr. Jim was his main man for expansion in the North. In 1889, Leander Jameson, pleased with his accomplishment as a go-between for Rhodes' dream, wrote his artist brother, Midge, "I close the books on my medical career. Sorry in a way, but I've gotten into too restless a way of life to settle down."

Restless and full it was for the next five years. He led colonists to what had been the Matabele's land. He organized villages, transportation, telegraph and police forces. He explored the boundaries of the Charter Company's lands, negotiating with tribes in territories held by Dutch and Portugeuse interests, occasionally inviting prison terms for his boldness. He established a small seaport on the Indian Ocean at Beira. He began the settlements at Bulawago and Salisbury, and they took the form of small cities. His medical knowledge languished, coming to life on few occasions. Once his companion and friend, Dr. Rutherford Harris, while swimming, was badly mauled by an alligator. His survival and return to health depended in no small measure on Jameson's skill. On other occasions he was called on to close wounds and perform amputations on his soldier-police as they put out fires, most of black on black forays. And this medical knowledge was self-serving. In 1891, he fell from horseback when on an exploration expedition, injuring his chest. On this occasion as often happened with such injuries, a recurrence of malarial fever came and bedded him as he waited for quinine to interrupt the cycle of parasite growth.

He led his police force to turn back a Boer trek into the Matabele land, and exhibited his powers of charm to entice

some of the venturing Boers to settle in the Company's conces-
sion-lands.

In late 1893, leading his 700 man force of trained farmers
and miners, he administered a damaging blow to the Matabele
presence. This action came about as discontent increased
among Lobengula's blacks. They continued their tribal rights
of raids on other tribes. Now, however, they had come to resent
the customs of settlers. Sometimes their raids washed over into
the lives of the settlers. Jameson led his crack team into the
village of Victoria and forced Lobengula's men to surrender
and be punished. Lobengula called the tribes to meet and
extract a price for breaking of the agreements. Jameson's reply
was attacks on the native kraals. Lobengula fled from his
former land and shortly after, died of smallpox.

In 1894 during a time of relative calm, the doctor took off
for a long postponed visit to his family and friends in London.
He was treated as a hero. Cecil Rhodes was there to enjoy his
company. No doubt, with Rhodes' influence, Queen Victoria
decorated Jameson with the Order of the Bath. At the Imperial
Institute he told of the coming federation of States under the
Union Jack (reflecting the many conversations of the Rhodes
"apostles" in Kimberley.) The news media cheered this as the
first hopeful news that had come from Africa in a long while.
A prominent British statesman, Earl Grey, said, "his exploits
as an administrator rival his exploits as a general." Some
doctor!

CHAPTER FIVE

Two South Africans, Prime Minister Cecil Rhodes, and his Company associate, Leander Jameson, M.D., C.B., arrived back in Capetown in February 1895. Both were pleased with the enthusiasm they found in London for the extension of English influence in the south of Africa. Both were ready to get back to this work. Jameson could hardly stem his drive, now steaming with praise for his newly demonstrated prowess to move people and things. Before returning to his duties in the north country, now officially named Rhodesia, he would visit his brother, Sam, a businessman in the still booming Johannesburg, in the Transvaal.

For more than a generation, the tip of South Africa felt the influence of two cultures, English and Dutch in origin. The Dutch Boers had come to settle on farms, and dig into the new land with a sincerity not manifested so intensely by the English, who went for trade and outside contacts with the rest of the world. The Boers were jealous of their hard-won prerogatives. It showed in their treatment of the foreigners who now swamped their cities. Jameson was shown the plight of the invader "Uitlanders." Though they outnumbered the Transvaal Boers in the jammed city, they had no vote, inferior schools, and were subjected to special and high taxes on food, supplies and other needs of life. Miners and businesses that supplied them, paid higher freight rates than Dutch and German firms. What the doctor observed reinforced Rhodes' expressions about the Rand, and resolved him to help remove Paul Kruger from power. Once "Oom Paul" was gone, there was hope for reform and even the longed-for joining of the Dutch and English colonies into a Federation of States. Furthermore, it was evident that Imperial Germany was cozying up to Kruger, and this boded no good for the thoughts of union.

Jameson was back in Salisbury in April 1895. Having the Transvaal reform movement in the back of his mind he worked on the Company's police force, increasing its size, and mounting a cavalry to better patrol the railroad and telegraph lines. About this time the company was given the task of managing Bechuanaland, west of the Transvaal. Jameson was ordered to Pitsani to assume the duty as Resident commissioner in July 1895.

Back in Johannesburg, the Uitlanders "reform movement" petitioned Kruger's government for new freedoms and were rebuked by a large margin by the Boer's Volkrand. Members of the Reform visited Jameson to be sure that, if they took up arms, they would receive support from the new force at Pitsani, Bechuanaland. They also went to see Prime Minister Rhodes at Capetown. He wore two hats. As head of a friendly nearby nation, he urged restraint. As the Chairman of the Charter Company, he was assuring the Reformists all the while, saying, "Keep the movement going and we'll keep Jameson nearby and ready if you need him."

During December 1895 the telegraph lines from the Cape to Jameson were busy carrying messages like, "hold tight," "don't play this week," "postpone the stockholder's meeting," "flotation must be delayed." The restless, confident, impulsive

Jameson, recalling how he made his own successful decision in the Matabeles had little tolerance left for the 'wimpy' Rand rebels. He was aware that leaks had informed the Boers that something was brewing. By year's end, Kruger would probably neutralize Jameson's force on the border. It was move, now or never. Once he bought that idea, no one, not even Rhodes, could keep him from going to Pretoria. The last man to visit him from the Rand was an old police friend, Sean Heany. He waited for a reply message from Jameson. The doctor left his tent, walked outside, musing and smoking two cigarettes. At last he reentered the tent and Heany asked, "What do you say, Doctor Jim?" Jameson replied, "I'm going in. What will you do?" "I'm going with you," quipped Heany. This was too good to miss.

CHAPTER SIX

Pitsani of the Southern Protectorate of Bechuanaland was a miserable place, treeless and barren. Jameson's contingent had ridden 1,000 miles in a month's trip from Bulawayo. Most of the men were fresh recruits, a few experienced soldiers, and fewer militarily trained officers. They were all for Dr. Jim.

Jameson, forty two years old, weighed just short of one hundred and fifty pounds, standing now with a slight stoop, a relic of his chest wound in the forest. He had a stubby chin, short straight nose, and a drooping black moustache. His wide-apart dark eyes came from under a broad forehead with a dark receding hairline. He looked as always as though he was about to say something he thought was funny. One old friend had said his eyes, "are those of an affectionate dog." This man had inspired Rudyard Kipling's

If you can make one heap of all your winnings
And risk it on one turn of a pitch and toss
And lose, and start again at your beginning
And never breathe a word about your loss.

At 5:30 a.m. December 30, 1895, Dr. Jameson, on a 16-hand black horse, got his troops together. He wore a civilian suit, a double Terai hat with the crown dented like a cup; he was covered with a fawn colored dustcoat with full skirts. There were in all 476 men and officers. Several mobile cannon rode with them. All telegraph lines but one were parted; the one left was a big mistake. It ended up in Kruger's Pretoria. The Boers made plans to greet the Doctor, unknown to him.

One of Jameson's friends in Johannesburg, an American doctor, Louis Wolf, had been charged with providing shelter, food and fresh mounts along the three hundred mile route. He was unable to get the job done. The Raiders had to stay on tired mounts. Few miles had been traversed before Boers harassed the effort. Instead of hoped for encouragement, the same words were heard from Boers and Reformists, "Turn back. Go back!"

On the second day of the ride, Kruger's grandson was captured. Refreshed, he was sent back with a request for a truce and a talk. On the third day—New Years Day 1896—less than thirty miles from Johannesburg, the Raiders reached Krugersdorp. Here Jameson found that the Reformists had worked out an armistice with Kruger and would not support the Raiders. Within hours the strongly armed Boers managed a perfect ambush in a deep valley near the town of Doornkop. Engaging in a close order gunfight, sixteen Raiders were killed and fifty six wounded. A white flag was raised, and John Willoughby, second in command, surrendered to Boer officers. Tired and shaking, Jameson dismounted. Sweeping off his curved hat, he said, "I surrender. I accept your terms." The infamous Jameson raid was at an end.

By morning, the doctor was in a Pretoria jail. Three weeks later, Jameson and his senior officers were handed over to the British Government at the Natal border, to be sent to London for trial. They left Durban on January 24, 1896.

CHAPTER SEVEN

Acheering throng was at the Bow Street police court in London on February 24, when Jameson and seven officers arrived. The mood of the crowd told of the thrill many people felt for the bold deeds of an Englishman against the dour German-speaking devils of South Africa. Jameson himself felt their approbation, and he appeared cocky and self-confident that what was coming would be a time of fun. The great wealth and influence of Rhodes plus the support he had found in the media a few years earlier would put to rest any concern for his acts being judged criminal. Out on bail, most were excused. But on the 20th of June, Jameson and four others came to trial on charges of violation of Neutrality Laws.

Not all of England supported the position of the then Foreign Secretary, Joseph Chamberlain[2] of the Conservative Party, in Queen Victoria's cabinet. Jingoes were proud of Kitchener, Gordon, and Rhodes as England's glorious empire expanded. But moralists opposed the use of force, backed by oratorical high-sounding religious phrases—the missionaries and "negrophilists" found plenty of media support to force an open trial in the Jameson matter. As the hue and cry rose, Rhodes and his advisors chose to stonewall the anti-jingo forces. The media event was colored by the number of the press who wanted the conservatives (Tories) torn from power. A select committee was appointed to determine if the Prime Minister of a British Colony (Rhodes) knew of Jameson's plans. They wanted to know if the foreign service representative in Capetown knew; they wanted to know what Chamberlain back home in London knew. It was a star-studded event.

The liberals had the smoking gun, a dispatch case of a Raider officer seized at Doonkoop by the Boers. In it were telegraph messages from Capetown to Johannesburg, plans to meet Jameson, and other damaging data suggesting Britain's involvement in attacking a neutral country. The special committee needed to break down people, and they did. But not Jameson. He simply said, "I did it on my own." Nor did they get Rhodes. His lawyer, Hawksley, never came up with the telegrams that were sure to have once existed, tying Rhodes to Chamberlain. Rhodes had the benefit of the writings of a lady reporter of the London *Times*, Flora Shaw, to plead for and protect him. And perhaps most of all a writer for the *Pall Mall Gazette* made the actions of the committee seem ridiculous. At this time W. T. Stead[3] became a close friend and advisor to Rhodes, helping to establish the Rhodes Scholarship Fund.

In the interval between his February arrival in London and the June trial, Jameson's shield of nonconcern turned to depression. He now saw his act as a betrayal of Rhodes' trust in him. No wonder he had not seen or heard from his friend. He aged before the eyes of his few loyal friends and his brothers. He was a worn out, forlorn, and thoroughly beaten man. He reluctantly answered questions. His position was, "I did it. No one else. Only me."

Jameson and four others were found guilty. The others were released, and almost immediately they returned to Rhodesia where the Matabeles, in the absence of Jameson's police, were again unruly. The doctor was sent to the Holloway Gaol, the old Castle near the school Leander had attended as a child.

Imprisonment was the least of his punishment. He had lost his best friend; he was cut off from the land he had come to love, and the chance to help make Rhodes' big dream come true. He was bitter, wanting to see no one. The bitterness was the same as a gambler's cry, "Damned bad luck. Had I succeeded I would have been forgiven. Losers pay." After a few weeks in Holloway he was operated on for kidney stones. His health failing, the Queen commuted his sentence and he was released to a nursing home, still sick in mind and now in body.

After more than a year's separation, Jameson, usually the mercurial one, had been confined and physically ill, condemned and beaten. Rhodes, the slow moving, stable one, still free but damaged, had turned to settling the Rhodesia rebellion and getting on with his dream. In January 1897, called back to testify before a select panel, he got the word on Jameson's sad state and went to the nursing home. "Both of us have had a rough time, but you, my friend, a rougher time than I." They embraced. The doctor began to mend.

CHAPTER EIGHT

Jameson's health improved and he gave some further testimony to the select committee in the spring of 1897. He was described now as a little man, "perilously fragile," but it was noted that there was a sparkle in his dark eyes and a smile about his mouth. He was still saying, "Everybody tried to stop me, but I went."

By August he was back in Rhodes' employ doing jobs in Rhodesia. Rhodes, temporarily ousted from control of the Charter Company during the trial and the investigation, had been restored. Back to work on his dream, he needed Dr. Jim for his medical care as well as a right-hand man. They worked together in Rhodesia; they vacationed together with an old friend, Beit, on the Mediterranean Sea and on the moors of Scotland; and fished with Willoughby in Ireland. The past troubles melted in the dream ahead.

Much against their wishes and in spite of efforts to prevent it, the Boer War[4] exploded in October 1899. Rhodes was trapped in Kimberley. Jameson, returning from a job in Rhodesia, was caught in Ladysmith, a small town in northern Natal. This pestilent town held 13,000 soldiers and 8,000 civilians, black and European. Food was short; there was a typhoid epidemic. During the Boer siege of the town, Jameson, detest-

ing idleness, turned to the care of the sick. For four months he
labored, losing many in his care. Desperately ill himself, he
was put on a steamer at Durban and taken, almost a dead man,
to Rhodes's hilltop home at Capetown, Groote Schoor, then
being used as a hospital. He left his physical strength at
Ladysmith. Thereafter he could be said to be an invalid.

Rhodes, liberated when the British lifted the Boer occupa-
tion of Kimberley, came to the Cape. Besides the pain of a fall
from a horse, he suffered congestion from heart failure. The
doctor was the more acutely ill, but the two shared a cottage on
the beach at Muizenberg, and slowly recuperated together. In
April, 1900, Jameson wrote his brother, David, "I'm almost
well again, and I'm going back to Kimberley."

As he promised Rhodes, he offered himself as a candidate
to the Cape Parliament from Kimberley. It was not an easy
choice, as he had to clean up the business about "the raid" in a
political arena. He was elected. He turned to the talk of
conciliation. He proved an able politician, and with the important friends of Rhodes meeting on the hilltop at Groote Schoor,
plans for the Union of States in South Africa slowly evolved.

In early 1902 Rhodes was forced to defend himself in court
against a little woman who had forged his name to documents.
The trial aggravated him. The pressure of his enlarging tho-
racic aneurysm on his lungs made him short of breath. The heat
of the days further burdened him. At the little cottage at
Muizenberg, he would sit on the edge of the bed, gasping for
air, and praying for a cool breeze.

Doctor Jim tried to answer his old friend's questions about
death. "Will it be clean and quick?" "Is it repulsive to others?"
The doctor would make a casual reply, but his voice would not
hold up. Rhodes would laugh then. "All Rhodes's wealth

could not have found him a better nurse," one of Rhodes's friends said.

Rhodes asked Jameson if his means were sufficient. In an airy way, Jameson said, "I've got plenty." When the doctor was out of the room, the sick man told his lawyer to provide for the doctor in his will. Jameson scotched that. As the end came, Rhodes said to Dr. Jim, "So little done. So much to do." He sang softly to himself and his friend. Jameson slept on a cot across from Rhodes's room. Rhodes died peacefully on March 26, 1902. His friends witnessed his burial in a granite tomb atop a Matopo hill. It had been a burial site of a tribal chief of old in Rhodesia. Rhodes had called it, "the view of the world."

CHAPTER NINE

Jameson had earned the forgiveness of his friend, and now turned to healing of old wounds among the Boers. By 1902, as he led the Progressive Party, he moved into the hilltop house. He became Prime Minister of the Cape Colony in 1904. He labored hard to bring Afrikaners into agreement with the British. Tiring of the effort, he resigned the job in 1908, writing his brother, Sam, "I'm coming back to London. Maybe some golf would give me a change and some rest."

Leaving the political field, he returned to become Chairman of the Charter Company. In 1910, the Union of South Africa, for which he had labored hard, came into being. In 1911, King George V gave him a Baronetcy. He moved into a large London house where he, and his brothers, Sam and Midge, shared their pleasures. On a late afternoon after golf Leander, smoking a cigarette and nestled into a chair before a roaring fire, would argue politics with his brothers. Sam would most often agree, but Midge would give him a good contest. The old doctor sat for Midge and the portrait resulting shows the brother's love and affection. The soft charm of his face is in marked contrast to the stern-faced portraits of Britain's other leaders in the National Portrait Gallery.

Gout came on to deprive his brothers of Lanner's presence on the golf course. Now his body, reduced to frailty, moved slowly. His face was masked by constant pain; his features more aquiline, his sad eyes more tolerant, his lips, covered by a gray moustache were smiling but not gay. He was a man, "enlarged by suffering, and having known humiliation."

Never one to shun duty, he accepted the job of directing the welfare of British prisoners of war in 1917. Paying the price of bodily damage over the years—malaria and dysentery in Matabeleland, typhoid fever in Ladysmith, renal stones in Holloway, injuries galore, intestinal obstruction, gout and now a neuritis giving him constant pain, he took to his bed November 16, 1917.

One morning Midge said, "Lanner, you look better." Jameson said, "No," and smiled. "Thank God, there is no hope." He died November 26, 1917 in London. He was buried in a local cemetery with an assemblage fit for a Pharaoh. He would have smiled at that.

In the *Bulawayo Chronicle*, Jameson's death was reported alongside the news that Mata Hari had been executed in Paris, the Battle of Cambrai was in progress on the Western Front, and a man named Lenin was making statements in Moscow.

In a time of peace, May 22, 1920, the remains of Leander Starr Jameson, M.D. were taken for reburial in a granite tomb at the right hand of Cecil John Rhodes, "in view of the world," atop the Matopo hill in Rhodesia. Symbolically, a patient and his beloved physician were together again.

"He had a personal gift. Trained as a healer, by genius a leader of men, in the old days in Matabeleland he commanded and doctored his Pioneers; he ruled and physicked his settlers. As in Kimberley, he looked with a surgeon's eye; he treated his adopted land as if it were a case of nerves, disordered by war, racial passions, and exhausted by the loss of blood. Such was the world of a good physician." (Colvin)

FOOTNOTES:

[1]Prince, a Canadian by birth, became a U. S. citizen just
as the war between the States broke out in 1861. He served
the Rebel cause and was imprisoned in Virginia as the war
ended. It is said he treated a fellow prisoner, Jefferson
Davis, at Fortress Monroe, Virginia. He became a doctor in
the regular army of the United States, but was suspected of
having tuberculosis. He resigned and went to the diamond
mines of Kimberley in 1870. In a native uprising here he
headed up his own troop, "Prince's Horde." He did this he
said so that he could say, "I served under two flags." On
leaving Kimberley in 1881 he retired to Durban, where he
was the American Counsel.

[2]This is the father of Neville Chamberlain, who also had
his father's position when one Adolf Hitler was claiming
territories as German in Austria and Czechoslovakia, and
being warlike in his actions. He hoped, rather than was
convinced, that his decisions "keep peace for our times." He
erred.

[3]William Thomas Stead, an apocalyptic journalist, never
did things by halves. Boiled over with enthusiasm about
Rhodes's philosophy, he brought powerful friends into his
circle. He got General Booth of the Salvation Army to help
settle unfortunates in Rhodesia. He felt the trial of Jameson
was an overkill and wrote a stunning parody, "The History
of the Mystery," which helped to draw the curtain on the
Committee's investigation. Stead, once jailed in Holloway
Prison for kidnapping a young prostitute to fill out a story he

was working on, will be seen again in the story of Dr. Frederick Cook.

[4]The Boer War that became inevitable furnished outstanding war news pouring out from war correspondents who became famous. In reading San Francisco newspapers of the Boer War times, 1900-1901, researching another story, I could not turn down the opportunity to read dispatches from South Africa by Rudyard Kipling, Richard Harding Davis, and Winston Churchill. And as I read, it depended on who was writing as to who appeared to be winning this intense and deadly conflict.

BIBLIOGRAPHY

Colvin, Ian. *The Life of Jameson* (2 vols.). London:
    Edward and Arnold, 1922.

Hole, H. M. *The Jameson Raid*. Bulawayo: Books of
    Rhodesia, 1973.

Pakenham, Eleanor. *Jameson's Raid*. London: Weidenfeld
    and Nicholson, 1960.

Williams, B. *Cecil Rhodes*. New York: Greenwood Press,
    1921.

A VERY INSUBORDINATE MAN

Leonard A. Wood, M.D.
1860 - 1927

Mt. Kisco, N. Y.
Aug. 5, 1927

To Doctor Harvey Cushing:
    I reported to General Wood at the cottage home of Mrs.
Katherine Mayo in Mt. Kisco, N.Y. about noon, July 30, 1927.
I enclose herewith a summary of my findings of the General's
medical history and a brief description of his physical condi-
tion. It is my hope that these will be useful to you when you
see him in surgery on August 6, 1927.
    The period of waiting with General and Mrs. Wood, and
sharing their bed and board, afforded me an opportunity I
seldom have with a patient, to listen and record things about
his life rarely expressed to a physician, mostly because there
is usually so little time for talk or for putting the record on
paper.
    For selecting me to attend the General, I thank you and offer
my notes to show my appreciation for this unusual event in my
life.

                        Forever Grateful

                        Caleb Coddington, M.D.
                        Intern, Peter Bent
                        Brigham Hospital

CHAPTER ONE

July 30, 1927

Medical History of Leonard Wood, age 67.

<u>Chief Complaint</u>. Numbness in left leg; numbness and tingling in left hand, and weakness in left arm. Swelling and soreness in right side and back of head, loss of power in arm and leg for almost one year.

<u>Present Illness</u>. Received a blow to the back of head as he rose from a chair and struck his head on a heavy brass chandelier hanging over a table in his quarters in Santiago, Cuba in 1898. Immediately a grapefruit-sized swelling rose into a soft lump. It subsided in a few weeks.

First noted tingling in fingers of left hand in early 1905 (almost seven years later.) On duty at this time in Philippine Islands, his active military duty was soon compromised by lameness in his left leg. In July 1905 was operated upon by Dr. Arthur Abbott in Boston, where a small benign tumor was removed from his right occipital region. Recovery was prompt and complete.

First saw Dr. Cushing in 1908 when the tumor seemed to have recurred. In late January 1910 while trying to scale a ladder at Governor's Island N.Y. he fell as his left arm seemed to lose strength. In February 1910, Dr. Cushing removed a

large growth from the right occipital area. Recovery was
prompt and the patient returned to active duty.

Symptoms of left-sided numbness and weakness returned in
the summer of 1926. Over fourteen-month period the condition
slowly worsened. He developed bilateral inguinal hernias,
undergoing surgical repair on the right in September 1926; the
left was repaired January of this year in Manila. While conva-
lescing, he was thrown from a car as it went over a small cliff.
Contusions resulted.

On board ship enroute to Boston, he was thrown from a deck
chair and suffered broken ribs on the right chest.

Past History. Usual childhood diseases. Had severe reaction
and abscess on right buttocks following tarantula bite in Arizona in 1886. Malaria attack, Santiago Cuba 1898. Severe
typhoid fever, 1901, beginning in Havana, Cuba and conva-
lescing on Cape Cod. Shrapnel wound left shoulder, 1917 in
France.

Family History. Father died at 65; mother at 81. One
brother, alive and well. Sister died at 11, rheumatic heart
disease. No history of cancer, heart disease, neurological or
mental.

Summary of Physical Examination. A large framed white
male, very well developed, large chest cage, heavy neck and
large head. Thighs heavily muscled; lower legs slightly
bowed and relatively spindly. Skin shows loss of elasticity,
and most of body exhibits loss of flesh. He stands with
slight stoop. His color is good. He is alert. Obviously he is
in pain from broken ribs on the right, which side is heavily
taped.

There is a large, oblong mass attached to the right occipital
bone. The mass is under his scalp and is slightly tender to

palpate. Other than bandaged ribs, heart and chest are normal.

He has somewhat reddened healing linear scars in both inguinal areas, no herniation. He has an indented rounded scar about 30 mm in diameter on his right buttock. There is a jagged scar over his left bicep muscle which extends over the deltoid muscle and into the base of his neck.

He shows loss of reflex action in his left bicep muscle and in the left knee and ankle. Some numbness is noted by diminution of tactile sensation in left arm and hand and left leg.

Impression   Intercranial tumor, left occipital area.

                   Generalized mild arteriosclerosis.

                   Fractured ribs, right chest.

CHAPTER TWO

The General was comfortably seated in an upholstered chair. He spoke with a deep voice and was very animated. He wanted to know where I came from. Where did I study pre-med, and where did I get my medical degree? What was my Dad's name? What did he do?

I finally convinced him that he was the main concern, and that I needed to know about him or, "my boss will hold me to account for omissions."

He was magnificent. From one question you could get a document for an answer. Further, as you shall see, certain of his old friends filled in the voids. He was an outgoing, frank and sincere person, and seemingly unaware of his great achievements. He expressed thankfulness for his past and enthusiasm for the future.

I mean to get my job done in the Islands. Then I can come back home and with Lou, my wife, enjoy the last happy days. So, doctor, get to your work with dispatch.

He seemed to enjoy telling of his boyhood. He was born in the little town of Winchester, N. H. in 1860. His father, Charles Wood, a part-time doctor and window-sash maker, took off to serve the Union Army in the South. The General explained that his father had, after longing to study medicine at Harvard, found it necessary to read medicine and attend an eclectic school in Pennsylvania to make the grade. It had not been a good enough education to get him a surgeon's commission in the Army but he went as a hospital officer. By his actions he won his commission on the hot battlefields in the deep South. On his return he moved to practice in Pocasset on Massachusetts Bay. The General reminisced—

My mom kept a warm and comfortable big house. They gave me a brother, Jacob, when I was five and a sweet little sister, Barbie, when I was eleven. She died early, and her passing was soon followed by dad's death. And, oh! I should not forget to mention that before they went, Miss Jessie Haskell, a schoolteacher, had come to live with us. I guess she helped to pay the board bill, but more than that she taught us to read books and keep accounts, and to learn to love all good things. I corresponded with her until I was almost 50 years old. My dad was great, but he kept so busy that we children hardly got time with him. Our mother was so strong that his passing meant only that our big house would be put to use to board travelers and transient fishermen. I got a lot of learning from people who went to sea for food. I loved the sea, and early on wanted to go to the Naval Academy, as I figured I could do well on a ship. After I finished the local Academy, I took a job on a fishing schooner, thinking that would be my career.

But mother and Miss Jessie had other thoughts. She got in touch with a neighbor, H. H. Hunniwell,[1] and he loaned me the money to go to Boston, and get into Harvard Medical School.

At age 19, Wood joined sixty other fellows in his class. It was a very scary start, and the raw lad from Buzzard's Bay avoided contacts for the first few days, spending most of his free time around the docks and eating only chowder. Some of his classmates were Brahmins from Boston, and perhaps a

fourth of the class were "hicks" like himself, from small towns
and little academies. Those were exciting days and what teachers they had: Oliver Wendell Holmes, Reginald Fitz, John
Homans and others.

*All of them inspired us. We had books to study at night, but
our chief education was to attend demonstrations and lectures.
You knew where you stood because each week you were expected to be examined before your peers and by your Masters,
standing up and being required to tell what you knew, what you
had learned.*

Camaraderie got them to plays and concerts and occasionally, as third year men, to cigars and hard drinks.

*I was so lucky. Liquor has not been a problem for me since
that year, when I fell in the Charles River in February. At the
end of my third year I had a job at the Boston City Hospital.*

In 1885, Leonard Wood was discharged from the Staff of
the Hospital.

*That was a real shock. I was sure that I was on my way to
success. I dreamed that I would get a staff appointment, maybe
even a faculty position at my own school—Harvard Medical
School, the leading school in the world.*

What had he done? He grinned.

I was insubordinate. Dr. C. H. M. Rowe,[2] *Chief Administrator at the Hospital called me up more than once for not
exactly obeying the rules. And finally he did not renew my spot
as a house officer, because I had catheterized a young patient
without asking my senior attending physician, and I had placed
a few small skin grafts on a young burn patient without checking with a senior.*

*The hospital work thrilled me. The patients were mostly
poor South Boston types. I remember reading Dickens at the
time, and relating my patients to the squalid London types in*

his novels. When I lost out at the City Hospital, these were the only people I knew to care for. The few months in my scrawny office brought me little income. I remember writing to Miss Haskell, and pouring out my soul on my condition. I used as a threat the possibility I might take the examinations to become an Army Medical Officer. She tried to suggest (she never stamped her foot) I wouldn't like it, but I went to New York in May 1885. Six days of examinations and tests, written and oral, on every subject imaginable. I was relieved to know that I had passed the tests, mostly to know that my bed and board was solved for a time.

Mrs. Wood set a table for our lunch in the shady corner of the screened porch. The General rose from the chintz-covered chair, and with an effort, straightened up. In spite of his painful rib injury and weakness in his left leg, he graciously bowed me into my seat. Mrs. Wood did not sit with us. Her Norwegian house lady served our soup and we were left alone to enjoy the food. It was a long luncheon as the General, with a sparkle in his eye, told of his first duty in the United States Army. He reinforced his account of duty in Arizona from 1885 to 1889 by giving me books, his memories of the Geronimo campaign and the memoirs of General Nelson Miles, to read in the evening.

To see the strong features, the lion-like head, and the craggy brows of the General, to hear him giving a deep voice to the amazing story, was a very unusual experience for me. A New Hampshire born, Cape Cod raised, Harvard trained doctor in the sagebrush and arroyos of the hot and dry desert of Arizona captured my imagination. Always a physically active youth, fond of rowing, swimming, and boxing, he volunteered to ride horseback, and hunt on every occasion. He was one of three medical officers at his post in Fort Huachua, and the only one of them who wanted to ride with the troops in pursuit of renegade Indians who almost constantly disagreed with the commands to live peacefully on the land reserved for them.

About the time the doctor was taking his entrance examinations in New York, three Apache leaders, Nachez, Juba and Geronimo went on a big drunk after which they and about 180 of their tribe—men, women and children—left the reservation. They fled to their mountain refuge in Northern Mexico. Constant Indian raiding took place over a wide area, and Wood spent almost a year doctoring troops and ranch families and living the nomadic life of a mounted soldier. He loved it.

Our way of thinking about putting an end to the chase of the guerrilla fighting Apaches changed in April 1886 when Nelson Miles took over from General George Crook. He was convinced (and maybe Henry Lawton and I helped in this) that American troopers could be trained to endure as well as the desert Indian; and by constant, unrelenting pursuit, Geronimo and his followers could be brought to the camp. He gave Captain Lawton the charge and I went with Troop B. We went thousands of miles and took almost eight months but we brought them in. Henry Lawton was about four inches taller than I, and outweighed me by fifty pounds. He was, like me, a fitness freak as I found out in a lot of boxing matches. He had one bad habit, boozing, and when it was being used, I had to get about three other troopers to help me get him to bed. But we made it. He had a terrible bout of malaria, and I got bit by a derned tarantula which abscessed and caused me to walk my horse for many a mile. But, we made it. Geronimo came in, and General Miles got a big promotion as that horrible Indian and his double handful of ragtag thieves kept the whole country on edge until they got him to the Florida prison. The Indian Wars just about ended there in 1886.

General Miles became an important and influential friend, yet with all his clout he was unable to get Wood transferred to his staff on the West Coast. Wood, as was his sense of duty, wrote to Surgeon General Sternberg, criticizing the diet and the uniforms of soldiers stationed in the Southwest. The General grinned. . . .

I should have kept my mouth shut. Even Miles couldn't get me moved out of the Arizona Territory after that. Duty there became routine and dull for a doctor. We had some social life on the post as the wives, daughters and visiting belles put on a party and music for dancing more than once a month. You could ride over to Tucson for glimpses of civilization, too. I began to aspire to command troops and to find a way for a more rapid rise to the comforts of rank and maybe a wife and family.

Mrs. Wood returned from her shopping. She shared with us ice tea with mint leaves. She bustled the General off for an afternoon siesta. I turned to my notes and the books the General had given me.

CHAPTER THREE

July 31, 1927

We had a heavy shower this morning. The breakfast room was cool without the fan. The General slept well after I had given him a phenobarbital tablet about 10 p.m. He walked steadily, and seemed more rested than yesterday. Mrs. Wood was with us for breakfast.

Young man, you have already, or will make, a contact that will make a big difference in your life. I could say that there will be more than one as I look at Lou (Mrs. Wood). *But I have reference to Nelson Miles. He really changed my life. He called on me in an emergency to tend him in California in 1887 when he broke his femur in a carriage accident. That was my first look at green and beautiful California, and I surely hated to have to go back to Arizona. Even though General Miles was ordered back East, he arranged for me to be transferred to duty in San Francisco at the Presidio. No Army post can be more beautiful than that. I have so much to be grateful for in that lucky appointment. First, it was at a dance at the Presidio I met this angel* (lowering his head and turning his gaze on the serenely beautiful graying Mrs. Wood). *Louise Condit-Smith was her name. She and her beautiful younger sister were slumming at an Officers' dance. Her guardian uncle, Justice*

Stephen Field,[3] *of the Supreme Court had permitted them to go with friends to the post and I saw her. I danced too. I think it was dancing.*

He smiled. Lou Wood interrupted.

Dr. Coddington—Caleb, if you will allow me—the occasion is vivid in my mind. My sister and I were born and grew up in Washington. My uncle was a Californian and it was our first trip west. We were constantly 'oohing' and 'aahing' at the beauty of the mountains, the hills, the Bay, the flowers and finally the handsome officers in their finest blue dress uniforms. Sister went off somewhere but I was caught, excitedly trapped, by a huge blond giant with a blond mustache and beautiful close-cropped hair. We danced, and I hardly noticed that he led me strangely. But it was much more thrilling to walk out on the grounds and down the walk toward the parade grounds. I tell you, no eighteen year old girl has ever been more overwhelmed by an almost thirty year old, hero soldier, doctor, would-be-dancer!

She laughed. At this point, the General took over:

I got to see her six times, I think, before the Judge packed her off, back to Washington. But she had my heart. It was here I met Lt. Frank Runcie as a patient, and he began to instruct me on how to become a line officer. The medical duties were attractive, as the ranking Medical Officer was tired and I got most of the good and interesting work. I had time to take up the new game, to me, of football. We had a good team on the post that competed, successfully I might add, with the University of California and other colleges along the West Coast. Boston seemed far away, the hot desert duty was barely a memory and paradise was at hand. I had better go get Lou and bring her here to make life complete.

Mrs. Wood set her shapely face aslant, reminiscing.

So he came to Washington in March 1890. We were married before God and the entire Supreme Court of the United States. From the moment he put his ring on my finger, my life changed. It became wonder, excitement, amazement, concern, worry and just pure happiness. And of course, along the way came the two boys and our dear daughter to complete our home wherever it was, from Arlington to Zamboango.

She laughed.

In 1893 Doctor Wood was assigned to duty at Fort Mac-Pherson, near Atlanta, Georgia. The medical duties here were not demanding so that Wood, avid as usual for things to learn or perfect, enrolled in a wood-working class at the nearby Georgia Technical Institute. This school was about to enter its second year in football competition. The doctor, loving the game, joined the team. He became the coach. At age 33, married and father of a baby boy, assistant surgeon at the army post, he also played ball. The team, playing the University of Georgia for the first time, defeated the Athens, Georgia team 22-6. "I actually scored four times—you only got 4 points then for a touchdown." The Athens fans claimed "the big ringer" had cheated them. The team, later called the Georgia Tech Yellow Jackets, dodged flying slats and stones and had a wild ride home to Atlanta and a heroic welcome.

Mrs. Wood added:

Atlanta was a nice, friendly place, but I was happy when, at last, Leonard was ordered to duty in Washington. General Miles was now Chief of Staff and even the Surgeon-General couldn't keep us away. It was so good to get back home. Busy, glorious days!

She smiled and her attractive face shone. She took the General for a walk around the hedge-enclosed yard.

CHAPTER FOUR

August 1, 1927

I had been up, had breakfast, walked around the yard, and on my return was greeted by General Wood.

"Great day, great breakfast." He passed both hands across his abdomen, and took up the telling of his duties in Washington. He was the physician on call to almost every important person in the town. Army people were his first priority, but from his post on the staff of the Chief of Staff General Miles, he saw Senators, Congressmen, Justices, Diplomats and many top bureaucrats. His friend, Runcie, though still ailing, was stationed in Washington and continued to fill Wood in on the requirements of a line officer. Charles Ainsworth,[4] had gone to the line and was already two grades advanced to a Major's commission. "That was another reason to want to become a line officer," he said with a grimace. Grover Cleveland was in the last part of his Presidency, and was not too kindly disposed toward Miles.

It was only in the late summer of 1896 that I was invited to go fishing with President Cleveland. We hit it off very well, mostly because of our mutual love for fishing or going out to get them. You probably don't know this, Caleb, but Grover

Cleveland had little use for William Jennings Bryan, did not give him the needed backing and, thusly, William McKinley, the Republican candidate, won the Presidential election of 1896 easily. His dear wife had never recovered her health after the loss of both her children. She became one of my favorite people and my patient. I saw her almost daily, and became close to President McKinley.

The pace of the times was being tainted by the dissatisfaction of the Cuban people with their Spanish rulers. The press, led by William Randolph Hearst, told of hideous brutalities, Spanish oppression and a bloody rebellion on the island so close to our shores. The feel of war, the smell of powder, was in the air, and Wood wondered if the time to become a line officer might be at hand.

If I hadn't liked to run and throw and kick a football, I might never have gotten to know Theodore Roosevelt. I met him at a dinner party in 1897. I learned he had followed the Indian Wars in Arizona closely, and had, as a matter of fact, proposed raising a volunteer group to go help the Army. Of course, I had read his great history of the west. It was a case of mutual fascination. We arranged to take our children to Rock Creek Park, where we played ball and picnicked. Those were great days. I was bigger than Theodore, but he made up with guts and desire and determination any lack of size or muscle. We boxed, we ran, we fenced, we rode horseback, we skied in the winter on sloping private yards. Lou and I became close to the Roosevelts. He was the soul of enthusiasm, a real tonic.

At that time, Roosevelt was Assistant Secretary of the Navy, bored and pushing for military action against the Spanish. Thinking alike, they talked of going to the Yukon to try the gold game.

On February 15, 1898 the U. S. Battleship *Maine* was blown up in Havana Harbor.

I was in the President's office two hours after the news broke and I told him I wanted to go to war. McKinley said, 'What war? I have seen the bodies of war and I don't want to see any more. You are our doctor, and you are needed here.'

I knew I wanted to be a part of the war that was coming. I felt that Theodore's political talents would find him a way of participating, and I would tie in with him. He tried to raise a volunteer army first in Massachusetts, then in New York, with no success.

Their chance came when the Governor of Arizona offered to recruit and pay for a mounted force of 'western cowboys' to go to Cuba. Roosevelt followed up on this lead and secured the necessary Federal backing for this effort. Leonard Wood was selected to recruit, train, and, as Colonel of U. S. Volunteers, to command the effort, Lt. Colonel Theodore Roosevelt to be second in Command.

I asked the General about his receiving the Congressional Medal of Honor.

No doubt President McKinley's giving me the Medal had a bearing on my being given the duty to train the mounted group. I got the Medal in June 1898 in the midst of war fever. It was given for duty in the Geronimo Campaign twelve years previous. Theodore was almost happier than I. I must say there were many who knew soldiers who deserved it more than I. I never once thought of giving it back.

At this point, Major General Frank McCoy arrived. He was greeted by Mrs. Wood as she would a son, with prolonged hugs and kisses on the cheeks. General Wood shook hands and was hustled off for his afternoon rest. General McCoy joined me on the verandah for a drink, settling in the bluish window chair.

*I first felt the presence of Leonard Wood on the football
field at West Point. He had come up from Washington to
referee a game we were playing with Amherst. I had just been
hammered by one of their tackles and it hurt me all over. I took
a good punch at his face, and the referee caught me. He
stopped the game. He simply destroyed me—kicked me off the
field. He did it in a way I'll never forget. I couldn't help but
cry, and I was glad to leave the field. He was such a presence—
big, strong, a commanding voice. Man, I was impressed.*

*Then, two years later, I looked up from where I was lying in
a cane field in Santiago, and here was the referee himself,
soaking wet with sweat, changing the wrappings on my right
leg. I'm sure he saved my leg and my life. A field medic had
applied a tourniquet too tightly. Here was a Brigadier General
worrying about a Second Lieutenant in the midst of shooting—
being doctor long enough to save a life. Richard Harding
Davis, reporting to the* New York Herald *at the time of this
battle, said,* 'Wood was one of the best examples I have ever
seen of the power of one man's authority to discipline soldiers.'
I'll buy that.

I asked General McCoy about the reputation the Rough
Riders had achieved in Cuba.

*Leonard Wood, relishing his switch from being an Army
Doctor, lost no time in putting the mounted volunteers together. He chose San Antonio for the assembly and training of
1,200 volunteers from throughout the Country. The press made
so much about the outfit that Theodore Roosevelt was in, that
it complicated its fulfillment of duty. Nonetheless it boarded
at Tampa and got to Siboney, Cuba in the middle of 1898. They
reported to Wood's old Geronimo Campaign boss, now General Henry Lawton's infantry division. Right away they moved
into battle, and they attacked Spanish entrenched on a ridge at*

Las Guardinas, and charged up what became known as San Juan Hill. Roosevelt led the way to drive the Spanish from their emplacements. It was the first big fight Americans were in, and the press ate it up. In less than a month the war was over.

McCoy healed from his wound rapidly, and was assigned as an aide to Wood, now a breveted General, and Military Governor of Santiago Province of Cuba.

During the next three years, I came to love this man I served as Aide. It was a task for a genius to convert the Spanish colony to the Republic of Cuba. As it has turned out, Cuba still boils and bubbles and revolves, but we gave it laws, courts and a constitution, railroads, schools and hospitals. Leonard Wood was its maker. In no way could I tell you of the divisions of interest in that Country—old Spanish customs and colonists who stayed and protected their power, clever mestizos who divided peons up into power packs, Yankee traders looking for exploitation chances, church leaders at each other's throats. It was the patient, strong Leonard Wood who sat them all through the time needed to draw up the rules and complete an election to succeed his Governor-Generalship. He was anxious and ready for it to come, and glad to return home.

McCoy traveled the world with General Wood. Twice he went to Europe with him for the War Games, in 1903 and later in 1912. Wood was a real professional, honored by his military peers in Germany, France and England. He was impressed by the preparations necessary for combat. He foresaw the coming war in Europe, and,

being what he is, he spoke out for America's need to modernize and get prepared. He paid dearly for this 'insubordination' when war came in 1917. The only politician who ever shared his concern and gave more than lip service to

Wood's concern was Theodore Roosevelt. By 1912, unfortunately, he was in the doghouse, politically.

General McCoy was worked up at this point. We had another libation and soon moved to the supper table, where the conversation got around to family intimacies. The love of the Woods for General McCoy, and its return was obvious.

CHAPTER FIVE

August 2, 1927

We had a morning shower, then the sun appeared to drive moisture to its intended places, making it a refreshed but warm day. The General was 'on top of the world.' How he could suppress the pain in the back of his head, I hardly know. The impression that all of his life he had been able to endure hardships came through strongly today. He stood.

Caleb, I have been a very lucky man to be so bullheaded. I blew my chance to be a respectable, Harvard doctor-professor. I got some awful first duties in the Army Medical Corps, and considering where and how I went, I'm lucky to be here. General Miles gave me a chance and liked me well enough to get me to fix his leg. He got me to Washington. I guess I should put Louise in my good luck circle. Could I have been luckier than having her for my beloved wife? Once in Washington, her family connections got me friends I could not have made otherwise, Grover Cleveland, and then President and Mrs. McKinley, good and loving friends. It was with his reluctant support that Theodore Roosevelt and I got our own regiment. President McKinley gave me the chance to give Cuba its new government.

The bullet of Leon Czolgosz cut down my friend, William McKinley, and brought Theodore Roosevelt to the Presidency. With all my luck I intensely desired the power to make the Army, which had become so much to me, to be the best it could be. That job is so big. It can only be accomplished by effort, constant effort, and continual awareness of human faults, laziness, sloppiness, greed, graft and all the other excuses for inefficiency. The new President was my closest friend. He was strong, a complete patriot—100%. He got me into the Regular Army, and to the top post. I never let him down.

I noted a change here. From a happy, bubbly start, his voice now had the sound of the threat of sadness and tears. I broke this train of thought by some medical talk. I asked—

General, as your military career evolved, how did you find your medical background—a help or a hindrance?

Well, now, that's quite a question. I think being a doctor helped me a great deal in my first duty in Arizona. The men on the base were served by several medical officers. That's why I was glad to go out on forays with the men. I loved the physical effort. I got to see ranchers and their families, as well as the troop problems. It got a lot of support and friendship in the Territory. It also got me in trouble as I wrote a long blast at Surgeon General Sternberg complaining of the bad state of the food and clothing issued for the troops. This probably kept me in Indian Territory for years longer than any other officers.

In Cuba my medical background helped me a great deal. When the shooting was over, the restoration of civil life in Santiago was principally to clean filth from the streets, to feed the people, and control diseases like dysentery, typhoid fever, and the like. To get clean water and enough food for the city, I got great support from the sanitary fellows, not only there, but all over Cuba.

*The greatest achievement of my whole life was the support
I gave to my fellow Army doctors led by Walter Reed. His boss
(and also formerly mine), Surgeon General Sternberg, did not
believe the mosquito connection with Yellow Fever. I broke
the Army routines, and as Governor gave the money Reed
needed to finish his experiments. Thank God! Reed's work
allowed us to remove the scourge of Yellow Fever from Cuba
and from the whole world. That's a privilege but few ever
get—to be a part of, even a little part of, such a big achievement.*

*It seems that wherever I have been stationed, disease is a
part of the scenery. Arizona with its Malaria and dehydrating
diarrheal disease; Cuba with Malaria, Yellow Fever, and the
dysenteries; the Philippines with its wide variety of exotic
tropical diseases and Leprosy in addition. This cottage, that
Katherine Mayo has so graciously loaned to me, comes about
for her interest in wiping out Leprosy from this world. You
perhaps know her for her famous novels.*

*Less than a decade ago we had the world pandemic of
Influenza. It played a deadly tune in our training camps, and
in civilian populations around the world. Being a doctor
helped me to deal with this problem in the camps.*

*To answer your question, I think my Boston training helped
me greatly from a policy standpoint. It did not give me any
great reputation for being a brilliant strategist, or even tacti-
cian in combat areas.*

He grimaced—a gesture of good humor.

CHAPTER SIX

August 3, 1927

Today we had a new visitor, Colonel George S. Patton, who had served as an Aide to the General both in the Philippines and at Fort Meyer, Virginia when Leonard Wood was Chief of Staff in 1910. He joined his old boss in the mid hours of the day, in part strolling slowly about the yard in spirited conversation. The General fatigued early, and the hard, compact, fit Colonel, dapper in his well-fitting blue jacket with gold buttons, good looking pale gabardine trousers, and dark brown cordovans, assisted him to an upholstered chair on the verandah. Later, after the General retired, I sat with Patton and we talked over drinks until dinner was served.

He spoke with the certainty of a Company Commander..

You see, doctor, a most remarkable man in Leonard Wood. He has but one purpose in life—do good for this Country. He breathes it. Never once have I seen him turn or quail from this position. I came here from Washington to see him. He was the only one ever there who I was really happy to serve.

To a man like him—Washington is a pit of snakes. The Adjutant General, Ainsworth in Wood's time—incidentally also a damned doctor—connived with Senators and other scum to oppose Wood's demands to close certain worn out posts fit

*only for fighting Indians who weren't there any more. He had
seen the German Army. My God, he knew what was coming.
He fought like hell and I went with him to reorganize the
various commands. He wanted airplanes fitted out for the
Army needs. We knew the Wrights could fly, but the asses
opposed that too. Members of Congress and dilettantes in Taft
and Wilson's Cabinets couldn't resist a chance to hurt
Roosevelt's buddy, Leonard Wood. Maybe it would have been
better if the General hadn't gone to Harvard Medical School
for a start. Certainly, Woodrow Wilson, a Princeton man,
thought the doctor had gotten too high in the Army.*

*But, by God, Wood was right in starting the training camps
and setting up the schedules for recruiting. We would have had
nothing in France without the start he gave us, opposed by all
the nincompoops.*

*I joined General Wood, then Chief of Staff, as an Aide in the
fall of 1914. He had seen the need to modernize from two
assignments to the War Games of Europe. As long as President
Roosevelt exercised any power he backed Wood and that went
through Taft's term. It was while I was with him that Wilson
came in and reversed the political threat. But make no mistake,
it was Wood's plan that Wilson's Chief, Peyton March, enforced. Otherwise we would not have been able to put a skilled
rifleman in France, much less a fighting outfit like the 89th
Division.*

It was easy to get strong opinions from this war hawk. He
deplored the treatment given to General Wood by President
Wilson and Secretary of War, Newton Baker. Wood, then the
ranking General, was relieved from duty as Chief of Staff, and
was not assigned to duty in Europe. General John J. Pershing,[6]
Commander of U. S. Forces in Europe was Wood's host on his
visit to Europe, where Wood was hit in the chest by shrapnel

during an artillery demonstration in France. Pershing saw him
in the hospital, but coolly refused to give him a combat assignment in Europe.

*One reason for this man to be forever honored is his sense
of duty and how, even though his Commander-in-Chief had
practically accused him of treason, and Newton Baker had
tagged him insubordinate, he bit the bullet; he swallowed the
bitter gall of rejection. He went to Kansas and trained the best
damned American Division to fight in France, the 89th Infantry
Division. Imagine his feelings, as the division arrived in New
York he was relieved of command! Stunned, and most certainly
entitled to react, damned if he didn't go back to the God-awful
Kansas plain and train the 10th Infantry Division. I'd bet my
best gun that that division would have been a great fighting
outfit too, had it a chance to get overseas. But—the war was
over.*

I turned Colonel Patton's attention to his earlier duty as a
young officer assigned to the Military Command in the Philippine Islands.

*I see my old boss, scarred by his long efforts, and hardly a
shell of the lion he was in 1905 when I first went to duty with
him at Mindinao. Can you believe it is now a quarter of a
century gone, and the damned Philippines are still not ready
to go on their own? Nobody—not even St. Paul—could have
been so patient and long suffering as Leonard Wood. From the
start—those Asian mixed-up masses would say one thing, do
another—agree one day and connive to knife you on the next.
Wood fixed the Cubans in less than three years. But, the
Philippinos—savage, questionable Christians, and Moslems by
professed faith defy the concept of self government. As Military Commander until 1908, and going back as Governor-Gen-*

eral in 1921, he has made his contribution and should get a big medal, and retire to a well earned rest.

But, again, this man can only go where he is driven by his inner spirit. When he came back from Cuba, the world of things was his to select from. He was rendered in oil by John Singer Sargent, and his old Arizona friend, Frederic Remington. He was famous. His best friend was President. Did he want to stay in uniform?? How about digging the Panama Canal? 'You need the money, an International group of Bankers are forming an organization that needs what you have— worldwide respect. The University of Pennsylvania desires you to become President. Pick one, please.' And then, Theodore says, 'Len, I need you to do me one more favor—would you go to the Philippines and put the military force there in shape to back the Governor-General Taft?' Sure, what else? Love of country. You know it.

I have enjoyed my day with the General. What do you think? Will he make it through the operation? He's such a great American.

This lean, tough soldier wiped his eyes. I thought I saw tears. He turned away.

CHAPTER SEVEN

August 4, 1927

I got the word today that Dr. Cushing was expected back from Europe on August 3, and that he would want the General in the Brigham Hospital on the morning of the fifth. A friend of mine, Alex Tribble, would be here before noon and I was to collect a urine sample and about 30 cc of blood to be taken to the lab in New York for a pre-operative study. I got these from General Wood.

About three o'clock Tribble left and a new visitor arrived, Kermit Roosevelt. I met him in the shady corner, my favorite part of the verandah. The General was napping, the afternoon was very hot, and the electric fan and cool iced tea made the interval conducive to conversation. Mr. Roosevelt was a small, slender man, with a dark heavy moustache. His face was not full like his father's, and he had an almost Mediterranean bronze cast to his skin. His eyes were dark under heavy eyebrows. He mused aloud.

Coddington, an unusual name. I know a Horatio Coddington—one of the few Horatios I have ever known. He's in a law firm in lower Manhattan.

"Yes, that's my father's brother. All of us are either lawyers or doctors. I got the harder part, I think, or at least the
better duty. " He continued.

*A warm day. I look forward to seeing the General. My
father and he were as close as any two men could be. My
recollections of the doctor, as we youngsters called him, go
back to the 90s. I remember a big snowfight we and the Woods
had in Rock Creek Park. Junior and I loved the nights we got
to spend at their house. Good food; great games. The doctor
was such a sport. He taught us football. He and father used
to box, fence and do all sorts of things together, and with us.
Dr. Wood was so big, so strong, stronger even than father,
though he would never admit it.*

*We knew and appreciated the doctor's great ability to get
others to follow his effort. Father said that all the glory that
came to him as a Rough Rider really belonged to Doctor Wood.
He put the regiment together; he led and willingly gave my
father the role of Richard Harding Davis's hero.*

*As a young man never forget that you have been blessed to
know a hero. His affection and loyalty to my father cost him
dearly. I think his one remaining unfulfilled ambition was to
be Secretary of War. In that position, he felt he might finally
have power to make the Army a pride to Americans. He had
never, he said, seen a determined effort to get that job done.
Also, politicians knew they could not push this man around. To
Wilson he was my father's pampered friend. To General Pershing, 'I do not want him in my Command. He can be insubordinate.' Presidents he served denied him the Secretary of
War's Cabinet seat.*

*The cruelest, the crowning blow to this good man was the
holding out to him of the Presidency of the United States, and
the contemptuous political assassination perpetrated at the*

Republican Convention in Chicago in the summer of 1920. No wonder my cousin, Franklin, decided the Democrats were more honorable and joined that Party. Many in the nation saw in Leonard Wood a way to correct the foibles and follies of the failing Woodrow Wilson. My father, sick, almost blind, and still shattered from the loss of my brothers, T. R. Jr. and Quentin during the war, had little political power left to offer his friend. As a fact, he caused Doctor Wood trouble politically as his many enemies in the Republican Party identified Leonard Wood with father's loathing of unconscionable business practices, thus moving them to other candidates.

At my father's funeral services in June 1919 Dr. Wood came away with the realization that it was he or Harding who would be the next nominee of the Republican Party, probably then President of the United States. And it was he who went to Chicago as the leading candidate.

He was first choice on the first eight ballots. A bitter, devious and dishonest charge of collusion with money interests of the East Coast made by Nicholas M. Butler, later Chancellor of Columbia University, sealed his fate. Warren Harding, a friend of the old guard, got the nod on the tenth ballot, a vote tantamount to being elected President. Wood, at last, expressed his bitterness in public, charging Butler with deceit and lying. To confirm what I have said of my friend, he stayed true to form, however wounded by the cruel realization that his character could not hope to be approved by political choice, and accepted from Harding a challenge to return to the Philippine Islands and bring them to the maturity of an independent nation. I have been there, and know the enormous task. Thousands of islands, a mixed group of races and people with a great penchant for terrorism. I understand that he is determined to get well and return there.

We talked of his condition, and I gave him my guarded opinion that General Wood was at serious risk. If it were another man, one not accustomed to making miraculous recoveries, I would doubt his ability to return to such a life as he had been leading in the Philippines.

Mr. Roosevelt spent a pleasant evening with the Woods and retired about 10 o'clock.

CHAPTER EIGHT

August 5, 1927

The General and his friend, Mrs. Wood, and I enjoyed a light breakfast. The lively conversation dwelt on the young hero of the day, Charles Lindbergh and his exciting solo flight to France. General Wood seemed just as excited about the feat of Richard Evelyn Byrd's flight to the South Pole. I even got them into talk about baseball, with the Yankees doing so well with Ruth and Gehrig. Mr. Roosevelt was going into town and asked me if I would join him at the game in Jake Ruppert's new stadium. I wish I could have gone, but I'll have to wait till a later date.

We are preparing to go to Boston this afternoon. I shall go in the automobile with Mrs. Wood and the General. He is in very good spirits. The General said, "I'll be back in Boston tonight. The Peter Bent Brigham Hospital wasn't there when I worked in Boston City Hospital. It's out near the new medical school, no?"

I affirmed this.

He continued, "I am so lucky. No one in the world is more skilled than Harvey (Cushing). He was the best neurosurgeon when he opened my skull fifteen years ago. Think how much

more skillful he is today! It will be like old times for him to
scalp me again.   Shades of the old Apache days."

*I want to thank you, Sir, for the vacation at Mt. Kisco. I am
forever in your debt for this chance to stay with a real American
hero. He is an inspiration to me. I pray for his safe passage
through the operation. I close these notes with that prayer.*

Caleb Coddington

CHAPTER NINE

Harvey Cushing, the properly acclaimed neurosurgeon, opened the occipital cranium of Leonard Wood. In the course of attempting to remove a tumor which had invaded the right cerebral hemisphere, encountered severe arterial bleeding from the right ventricle, which could not be stanched. Though blood transfusions and attempts at hemostasis were done with consummate skill, the patient died in the operating room.

At the end of many travels, strong demanding duties in far away places, situations hardly predictable from his Pocasset origins, he came to rest on the bosom of his birth. He is a man to be honored, a credit to the profession he left, and of the country he never failed. Insubordination in him was a virtue.

FOOTNOTES:

[1]A classmate, Dr. Frederick Jack, asked Hunniwell, "Of the many you helped to an education, how many repaid you?" He replied, "Only Leonard Wood. He was the only one."

[2]On Wood's leaving the hospital gates, Dr. Rowe is said to have remarked, "There goes a young man who will never make his mark." Much later, Rowe commented on Wood's dismissal. "At the time we did the right thing, but in truth, Wood was morally correct."

[3]Cyrus Field, financier brother to Justice Field, was responsible for laying the first trans-Atlantic Cable in 1858, among other achievements.

[4]When Leonard Wood was Chief of Staff, General Ainsworth was the Adjutant-General of the Army. He joined Woodrow Wilson in trying to cool down the ardor Wood had for closing outdated bases, and reforming the Army to meet standards Wood had observed in the armies of Germany and France.

[5]Citation for the Congressional Medal of Honor given Leonard Wood. Issued to Wood, April 8, 1898:
"Voluntarily carried dispatches through a region infested with hostile Indians, making a journey of 70 miles in one night, and walking 30 miles the next day. Also, for several weeks while in close pursuit of Geronimo's band and constantly expecting encounter, commanded a detachment of infantry which was without an officer, and to the command of which he

was assigned upon his own request."

⁶John J. Pershing was known in Indian fighting days as Black Jack from his duties with a largely negro cavalry unit in Arizona. Wood had assigned him the duty to handle Pancho Villa in 1914. Wilson selected Pershing to head the U. S. effort in France, probably aware that Pershing's father-in-law was a prominent Ohio Senator, John Sherman, younger brother of William T. Sherman, and renowned for the Anti-Trust laws that bear his name.

BIBLIOGRAPHY:

Hagedom, Herman. *Leonard Wood, a Biography.* New
    York: Harper Brothers, 1931.

Wood, Leonard. *Chasing Geronimo.* Ed. Jack Lane.
    University of New Mexico Press, 1963.

Faulk, Odie B. *The Geronimo Campaign.* Oxford Press,
    1969.

Creekman, James. *The Doctor Who Became a General.*
    Pearson's Magazine, April 1909.

A LIAR AND A GENTLEMAN

Frederick A. Cook, M.D.
1865 - 1940

CHAPTER ONE

The winter blizzard of 1888-89 brought a paralyzing snowfall never equalled in New York City's history. All traffic in the city was halted. Theodore and Fred Cook, young men in their twenties, put their horse-pulled milk delivery trucks aside, pulled a skiff from the East River, and fitted it with runners. Soon the brothers were delivering coal to shivering shut-ins over the city. Their ingenuity got them the attention of the city readers of Leslie's magazine.

The "get up and go" of these brothers was no surprise to their family or friends. The widow, Magdalene Cook, had brought her children back to Brooklyn after her husband, Doctor Theodore Koch (later anglicized to Cook), died in a town near the Catskill mountains. She and her daughter took in sewing for the sweat-shops of the day. Ted, the oldest boy, got a job with a beer barrel maker. The younger two boys found work in Fulton's Fish Market across the East River in Manhattan.

Many heroic tales of American settlers involve little cabins in the forests of Appalachia, or in shacks on the Continental Divide. But a picture of 13-year-old Fred Cook, his 11-year-old brother Will's hand in tow, riding across on a ferry boat at two o'clock in the morning, speaks of bravery. Especially, heading for work in a huge Metropolitan market to face fiercely competitive, endless haggling, horrendous disagreements, things stressful to adults much less children. These were real lessons in living. In spite of the hours, the boys kept up with their schooling.

Fred wanted to be a doctor, as his German immigrant father had been. The close knit, hard working family could cheer for that, but the money, even by a gang effort, was not there. He bought a second-hand printing press on which he created stationery headings, billing forms, and advertising, selling his wares at shops on the way to the ferry and around the fish market.

As he finished high school he put together a door-to-door milk delivery system for the new-fangled quart glass bottles. His brother, Fred, helped him build a special wagon to be drawn by horses. Soon there were more wagons, horses and drivers. Cook now had the means to enter the College of Physicians and Surgeons at Columbia University across Manhattan Island. He worked a long-houred day, rising at 1 a.m. He checked his men at the depot, and if a driver were absent, took a route himself. At 10 a.m. he was at the medical school, attending lectures on the action of drugs, discourses on the functions of the body's organs, anatomy, chemistry, and ending the day in body dissections about 5 p.m. He went home and prepared for the next day's demonstrations and exams, totaled up his milk accounts, solved problems, ate, and slept till 1 a.m. came round again.

At the end of the first year he transferred to the Medical College of Bellevue on the East Side. In 1889 the blond, handsome, blue-eyed man with a solid athletic build grew a closely trimmed beard to better fit his soon-to-come medical degree. At a church social he met Elizabeth Forbes, a lady

stenographer employed by the shoe manufacturer French, Shri-
ner and Urner. They married in the spring of his graduation.

In the early winter of 1890 a double tragedy struck Cook.
The great joy of becoming a doctor was wiped out by the death
of his wife. Being delivered of her first child, she suffered
tears in the process, and the ensuing peritonitis killed her. The
child, born dead, was an added blow. Bitter and bewildered,
he wrapped himself in the solace and comfort of his loyal
family. His mother and sister, Lillie, moved into a Manhattan
home in the basement of which the young doctor opened his
office. The milk and coal delivery business was sold to his
younger brother, Will.

The scarcity of patients gave Fred abundant time to read.
He was enthralled by a current hero, Elisha Kent Kane, United
States Navy Surgeon, who had gone into the frozen Arctic in
search of Sir John Franklin's lost expedition. Kane wrote of
thrilling trips over vast expanses of ice; of Eskimos, dogs,
desertions and mutinies; fights with crews and natives, hazards
to health, snow blindness, frostbite, fractures, all told by a
medical man. "What a place to be, to forget your other cares."
Cook was lost in thought.

He also read of Charles Francis Hall, a printer (Cook had
done some of that, too) who followed up on Kane's last trip to
Greenland. In Hall's account, another doctor figured promi-
nently in the work of the mission.

Here was a man, trained in medical science, anxious and
lonely, and waiting for a chance to put his mind and skill where
someone needed him. He read a notice in the New York *Herald
Tribune* in early 1891. Lieutenant Robert E. Peary of the
United States Navy, preparing for an Arctic expedition, sought
a surgeon to sign on the voyage. Dr. Cook sent an application
by mail. Two months later he hurried by train to Philadelphia.

He met Peary; they suited one another; Cook signed on. He became the expedition Surgeon and ethnologist, the latter designation on Peary's say-so, no doubt, and probably by default. At any rate, he was a doctor who was needed even if patients in Manhattan had not discovered him yet.

CHAPTER TWO

In June 1891 the vessel *Kite* sailed from Brooklyn commanded by Peary, and bearing his wife, our Doctor, Lars Astrup—a skiing champion, Leland Gibson—brother of the popular painter Charles Dana Gibson, Matthew Henson—a husky, black, body servant of Peary, and nine assorted scientists. On nearing Greenland, the vessel struck ice, and Peary, who was at the wheel, was dashed against the deck-house. He suffered a compound fracture of both bones of his leg. Almost the first event out of the gate was to try the surgeon. Cook was up to the task. He set the bones, and provided a cast which not only aligned the bones for healing but provided buffers against the frequent shocking blows of the vessel as she lurched with the weather. Peary was to say later:

10 months after I broke my leg, I went on a 1200-mile tramp on snow shoes, proof of the professional skill of my surgeon, Dr. Cook.

The party got off the ship on the west coast of Greenland, and constructed a shelter 21 feet long, 12 feet wide, and 8 feet high. In this structure, called Red Cliff, Perry and his missus, and all the others, stayed for the long year.

As the lame and determined Peary hobbled around, preparing for the trip northward to discover whether Greenland was an island, Cook looked to the health of his companions, and found a lot of time to do other than doctoring. He traveled with parties on hunts for game. Peary wrote of the short time of instruction it took Cook to become the best shot in the group. Astrup paired often with the popular and amiable Cook on forays, and gave the doctor lessons on the use of skis and snow shoes.

Peary, limited for a while by his injury, gave the eager doctor lessons in the use of the sextant and compass. Cook, already a proven innovator from boyhood, worked with the older, experienced ice-traveller in fashioning sledges and harnesses for the dog teams. It was a time of learning for the doctor with his soft approaches and his agreeable manners. His tact was often called upon to keep the group from outbursts of resentment to the lady of Peary's choosing in the confinement of the little house, Red Cliff.

In addition to the scientific skills he learned and practiced, Cook took seriously the bogus title, "Ethnologist," that Peary had bestowed upon him. He met and made friends with Eskimos and slowly built up a vocabulary. The Eskimos accepted him, allowed him to measure their physical attributes, and to photograph them. He wrote voluminous notes on their diets, lack of infectious illnesses, their family habits, taboos and other social data.

He saw no scurvy in these people. He likened their bodily form to some of the Arctic mammals, particularly their small stature, compact bodies, short limbs, and fatty deposits, all seemingly designed to limit heat loss. He attributed their health and vigor to a diet of raw meat and fish. He noted that the spiritual as well as physical life focused on the sun. The souls of men lived in their shadows. Sexual activity came alive with the rising sun that put the long winter darkness away. The sun's coming inspired physical contacts, hunting for food and clothing, and replenishing the stores for the next winter.

Cook was left in charge as Peary and a small group took off northward. Henson had to turn back as he suffered a badly frostbitten heel, which the doctor successfully handled. Peary found the cliffs that proved Greenland to be an island. To the joy of almost all, and the relief from the social strains of Red Cliff, the expedition packed up and sailed south in the summer of 1892.

The comrades, on reaching Philadelphia, spoke enthusiastically of an early return to the Arctic. As a gesture of his generous nature, Dr. Cook was concerned about the damaged eyesight of Matt Henson. He took the stout-hearted black with him to his mother's house in New York. Recognizing his limited knowledge of the eye, Cook had an expert ophthalmologist care for Henson for two months before he rejoined Perry.

The 27-year-old physician moved his office to Brooklyn, where his newly acquired prominence spurred his practice. He was thrilled to be invited by the Kings County Medical Society to address them on his Arctic experiences. The presentation was a scholarly account of the physical and social characteristics of Eskimos, living away from civilization.

In the meantime, Peary was hustling support for a return to the Arctic and a try at the "furtherest North." He, too, had moved his home to be nearer the Brooklyn Navy Yard. He wanted Cook to sign on again as Surgeon. What a conflict! His practice was beginning to demand his attention. Now came the tempting offer to be an Arctic Explorer. He went to see Peary about publishing the lecture he had given; Peary refused permission; all stories of the expedition belonged to him as leader. Cook found this attitude too restrictive, and he recalled the general dislike of Peary, maybe generated by his demanding wife, in Red Cliff. He chose to continue his medical practice. That the separation was friendly was demonstrated when Peary asked Cook to do physical examinations on the members of the 1893 expedition. Cook was on the dock as his old companions sailed. The press reported that Peary regretted that his former surgeon, "cannot go along."

It was in the summer of 1893 that Cook again heard the call of adventure. Having dreamed as he doctored, he made it real by chartering a ship in mid-summer. He closed his practice and took off with a few companions to Greenland. It turned out that the Captain of the schooner was not adventurous and the 'scientific' foray was little more than a visit to Eskimoland and the Greenland fjords. There seems to have been no unpleasantness, and Cook got back to his patients.

By the following summer the busy doctor had another scheme to sell. This time he proved that the North Ocean appealed to young men in the East. He sold berths on a summer adventure to the north aboard the chartered ship *Miranda* at $500 a head. Fifty-five students from Yale, Harvard, Oberlin, Williams, University of Pennsylvania, and elsewhere sailed on July 7, 1894. Even at the dock the ill-fated *Miranda* had a collision and it was back to St. Johns, Newfoundland for repairs. On resuming their voyage, they had a collision with an iceberg and it was back again to St. Johns for repairs. The *Miranda* proved to be a certifiable 'collider' as on August 9 they bashed the vessel on a monster iceberg. The indomitable leader, Cook, took off with an Eskimo travelling 100 miles over cold open water in a small boat to bring relief to the foundering *Miranda*. The rescuer, a Gloucester fisherman, took the bewildered group to Sydney, Nova Scotia and safety. The adventurers got back in September, 1894. Probably as a tribute to the affable, unflappable, intrepid doctor, they formed the Arctic

Club of America to memorialize the trip of the doomed *Miranda*, and to tell tales.

The two summer distractions did nothing to lessen his practice and the good life in Brooklyn. His peers commented, "Skill, compassion, and an exceptional bed-side manner got him loyal patients and friends." There was an intrusion of domesticity in the coming wanderer. He became engaged to marry Ann Forbes, sister of his lost Mary. She was interested in the doctor, and in his life, and very much concerned about the far-away places of his dreams.

Fate would doom this pairing.

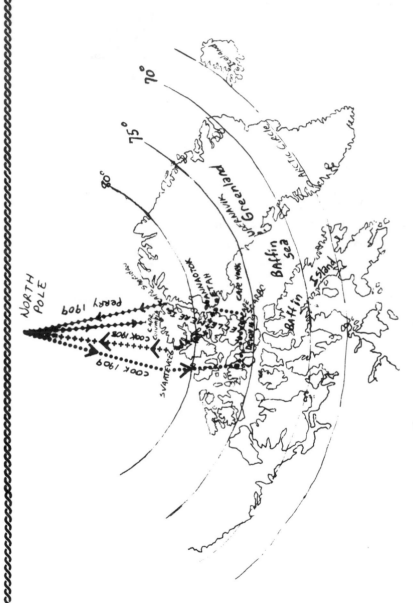

From Cook's Map Of His Journey

CHAPTER THREE

In August 1897 a Belgian Antarctic Expedition was reported in the *New York Sun* to be in search of a surgeon. Cook wired Brussels and three weeks later, his cheeks moist with the salty tears of Ann's goodbye, he took off for Buenos Aires, Argentina. Here he met the Belgian leader, Adrien de Gerlache, and boarded the *Belgira*. He, the lone American, had joined a polyglot group—Belgian, Scandinavian, Polish, Russian and Roumanian. Seven languages were present. Accounts tell of the doctor who saved the sight of a small boy as they paused at Tierra del Fuego. The *Belgira* dallied a bit before proceeding southward on an attempt to set the record for nearest the South Pole. It turned out to be a bad judgment call.

The mate on the *Belgira* was Roald Amundsen, who 14 years later would be the first to reach the South Pole. This man was honored and respected over the world for his achievements. In his account of this voyage, he paid the highest tribute to Dr. Cook for his help in the *Belgira*'s return from an amazing year trapped in the Antarctic ice.

A good doctor, with healthy officers and crew, is expected to turn to other duties and, if he is lively, to other opportunities. Food, of course, became a problem as the ship became imprisoned in the frozen sea. The good shooting doctor did his part to provide fresh meat and birds. Again, among men who knew navigation, Cook was a student in measuring distances, direction, and calculating positions. He took a photograph of the entrapped ship in the moonlight of an antarctic night, using a 90-minute exposure. This photo speaks volumes on the doctor's knowledge of photography. He was with men who used sledges to move, and Cook derived experience and ideas for their better construction.

As their captivity lengthened, scurvy hit the men. The doctor's faith in the foods the Eskimos of the north ate, got the reluctant crew to eat raw liver and meats in place of the ship's supplies. They recovered. He noted during the long year of close isolation a condition of pallor that he called 'polar anemia'. Almost all who suffered it ended with snow white hair. This, too, vanished as the contents of penguin stomachs was added to the polar diet.

The great challenges to survive the long Antarctic night came in the pent-up urges and despair, and in maintaining hope to escape the ice. In spite of the good doctor's efforts, three sailors departed from reality. At different times all would suffer from being cooped up. The wind, the cold, all discomforts, bore down on the spirits and the will to eat, or get up and move during the eight-month long night. The sickest ones underwent Dr. Cook's regimen—fresh food, exercise, artificial heat therapy, and low humidity. The heat therapy was a naked body by a roaring fire for at least an hour a day while the doctor shoveled up and fed the fire. Amundsen wrote:

During the 13 long months in which almost certainty of death stared us steadily in the face, I came to know Dr. Cook intimately and to form the affection of him and the gratitude to him which nothing could ever cause me to alter.

As he moved to cheer his mates, Cook also devised a scheme to chop a channel through which the ship might be released from its imprisonment. It was a tremendous feat of endurance for the men who helped, often cutting through eight-foot deep ice. And as the ship moved, it would feel the crunch of the shifting slabs. Dr. Cook was credited with tying penguin carcasses on the sides of the ship to cushion against the crushing ice pressures. A fortunate shift of winds helped shove the ship in a direction which freed its way to a channel that had once been a quarter of a mile away. The *Belgira* was freed to fire up her boilers and steam to freedom.

On reaching Montevideo, Cook learned that Ann, his betrothed, had not survived his long absence. The ship returned to Antwerp and Cook was knighted and presented a gold medal by the King for his contributions to the Belgian Antarctic Expedition.

Back home, he mixed his practice with the writing of his first book, *Through the First Antarctic Night*, published in 1900. The fame of this book gave another boost to his practice. (The book was republished in 1980 as a classic in polar descriptions.)

CHAPTER FOUR

The 1893 expedition that Cook refused to join had not been a successful one for Peary. Never beaten, he doggedly put together funds for another try. By December 1898 he, Matt Henson, and a Doctor Dedrick among others, went far up on the top of Ellsmere Island, a large land mass west of Greenland, in another attempt to get to the North Pole. In the bitter cold Peary froze several of his toes. On removing his shoes, the frozen toes snapped off at the joints. Dr. Dedrick, under very bad conditions, mostly imposed by his patient's behavior, saved what he could of that angry and frustrated explorer's feet. After six weeks, the party returned to the base camp. Here Dr. Dedrick left the expedition in disgust. Peary, the gutsy one that he was, learned to hobble on his single-toed stumps. He stayed in the camp for two years planning his move to the Pole, but with little progress.

Herbert Bridgman, an accountant for a Brooklyn newspaper, and a great fan of explorers, organized a relief expedition for Peary. The promoter was a backer of Peary and at this time also of his fellow townsman, Cook. Bridgman had accepted the hospitality of Cook's home at times, and he knew that Cook was held high in Peary's esteem for his medical talent. In spite of Cook's prior rebuff by Peary he did not refuse the request to help the suffering explorer. Bridgman's ship, *Erik*, got to Peary's camp in August 1901. Cook, facing his old boss for the first time in almost ten years, found him "wrecked in ambition, physique, and in hope." In addition to his maimed feet he was suffering from pernicious anemia.[1] Cook told Peary he must, if he stayed in this land, "eat raw meat and especially liver." Peary replied, "I would rather die; besides, liver is poison." Cook returned home in the fall, probably happy at having had another taste of his favorite form of diversion, the Arctic.

In the fall of 1901, on one of his now frequent travels, he met the attractive Marie Fidele Hunt, widow of a well-known Philadelphia surgeon. They married in June 1902. They cherished her cute four-year old daughter, Ruth.

Now he had another chance at domesticity—a wife and a child to work for. He gave up his horse carriage for a new-fangled Franklin car that ran on gasoline. He bought one of the first X-Ray machines used in private practice. His practice abounded. Marie and Ruth were accustomed to some elegance he had not thus far had time for. So they moved to an imposing four-story house in the fashionable Bushwick area of Brooklyn. They entertained not only friends in medicine and the neighborhood, but also New York's active explorers. The fourth floor of the house was a dance floor. This was high ground for the little boy who had crossed the East River long before dawn each day to his job in the Fulton Street market.

In the news came the description of the high peak in Alaska named for the recently martyred President, William McKinley. As Dr. Cook and Marie talked, he began to fantasize about the mountain, and how he would like to explore the area. He had ideas of sledge construction he had worked on with Amundsen. He thought of ways one could lessen the bulk and weight of food, clothing, and shelter so critical in survival, and in the success of travel in hard, cold climes.

He found David Abercrombie in lower Manhattan, in a shop specializing in the needs of hunters. Abercrombie recalled the first visit of Cook. "I thought I knew all about weather barriers, but he wouldn't have it." They remained friends for life after this start. Abercrombie responded to Cook's many suggestions with innovative products.[2]

Cook found he could get an advance on a book describing Mt. McKinley. At the Arctic Club and Explorer's Club he found men to join him. Among them was Ralph Shainwald, an Arctic enthusiast as well as a wealthy merchant who became his friend for life. A journalist, Robert Dunn, would pick up his part of the cost. They signed on a photographer and a horse wrangler. In May 1903, putting little Ruth in safe hands, Dr. and Mrs. Cook took off for Seattle.

Marie Cook's fun was short-lived as the rigors of the far west and the fierce summer mosquitoes caused her to retreat to the coast. The rest of the party moved in to try for the summit. From late June to mid-August the five men and their horses looked for a route that might go to the top of the mountain. They travelled completely around the massive monster on foot, by boat, and raft, almost 500 miles. With early winter closing in they returned and came home without climbing the mountain.

A fellow practitioner of that time spoke of Cook. "He was interested in the sick, generous in giving medical services in remote parts of the city, and in going to the local medical society." Marie brought home from the hospital a new girl baby, Helene, in 1905.

Mt. McKinley stayed on his mind. "There must be a way to stand on the top of America." When David Abercrombie did not come up with the right kind of sleeping bag, Marie sewed a three-ply cover—cravenette, camel's hair, and duck, each of which could be used separately as a poncho. This time the two little girls required that Marie stay home, not too difficult a choice for her. Cook and some high placed adventurers came up with the funds to go back to the mountain.

In May 1906 on an expedition to Mt. McKinley, ten men made a move to the base of the mountain. Among the adventurers was a Columbia professor as co-leader, an artist, a skilled topographer and Arctic veteran, a cook and two horse wranglers—one from the 1903 effort. The group spent several weeks trying to find a route to ascend to the peak—no luck! The professor gave up, agreeing that he would join another try, and so did the others. They turned homeward.

The account of the struggles of Cook and his horse wrangler, Edward Barrill, up a huge glacier, hacking steps up the icy face, was given in his next book (published after Cook had taken off on his polar adventure.) It was an exciting story in which he again showed his medical background, describing at some length the effects of high altitude and cold on the human mind and body. Each day's ascent was a lesser distance, but the two men reached the peak alone.

On the descent they encountered two mountain men who had survived a capsizing of their boat by clinging to icy rocks for days. Weary as Cook was, he spent hours doing the necessary surgery; dressing and caring for the pair. He and Barrill got them to a safe haven and proceeded down to Seattle, where Marie and Ruth gave him a welcome surprise. They were home by December, 1906.

His magazine articles and his book, "To the Top of the Continent," were well received by all but the Columbia professor who had helped raise funds for the venture that had climaxed without his knowledge or understanding of the plans of Cook. But Cook had made an outstanding journey, and again demonstrated his ability to adapt his sturdy body to conditions of high altitude, cold and ice. He had an insatiable desire to achieve. The book commented accurately on the great mountain and its difficult-to-conquer attributes.

It was almost impossible now to return to his successful practice. He and Marie went to Washington where the National Geographic Society honored Cook and Peary at an annual dinner; their last friendly encounter. This was toward the end of the year 1906.

CHAPTER FIVE

I n early 1907, while visiting his friend, David Abercrombie, Cook encountered John R. Bradley, a hunting enthusiast, good customer, and good friend of the merchant. Bradley listened to the spirited exchanges concerning cold weather gear between the noted explorer and his supplier. Bradley and his more famous brother, Colonel E. R. Bradley, had accumulated big winnings in Texas gambling and at their famous casino in Palm Beach. They had extensive interests in horse raising and horse racing. Otherwise, they went separate ways, the Colonel for Derby winners; John to big game hunting.

At lunch, soon after this meeting, Cook and Bradley planned a seal and bear hunt in the North. Cook found a ship in Gloucester, Massachusetts and had it prepared for an icy trip, having agreed with Bradley that without any fanfare, this ship might be going to a camp aimed at the North Pole. They looked for help, got a good Captain and crew, and Cook hired a young sturdy German, Rudolf Franke, as a steward. On June 3, 1907, the ship sailed from Gloucester.

The ship, the *Bradley*, arrived at Etah on western Greenland's coast in early August. Cook and Franke found the Eskimos and dogs they would need and put the natives to work assembling sledges, boats, food, and clothing for a later trip. Bradley got the hunting he desired, and agreeing that Cook should have a go at the Pole, he sailed back to New York. He took a message to Cook's Brooklyn 'friend,' Bridgman, now the Secretary of the Explorer's Club: "I will try for the Pole," and that he hoped to be back in about a year.

The winter spent in and around Annoatok was used in building sledges designed by Cook and his brother, Theodore, using hickory wood cut from the latter's New York farm. He and Franke hunted for meat and furs. The pelts of foxes, wolves and seals, and the ivory tusks of the seals would be sold to provide funds that Cook needed to defray some of the expenses that Bradley had underwritten. They assured themselves of good sled dogs. Cook had made a careful study of the maps of prior explorers. His final route was backed by the stories of Eskimos who knew the country where musk oxen carcasses would be collected, processed, and stored for the long return. This was a route over the top of Ellsmere Island, going west and northward to Svartevoeg. Cook would leave the land at a point about 500 miles south of the Pole. As the sun came to give notice of the end of the long night, Cook left Annoatok with Franke, nine eskimos, eleven sleds, one hundred three dogs, and his supplies.

After several days Franke was sent back with instructions to guard the supplies, the ivory, and the furs stored at Etah. "And Rudy, don't wait for me past June. Get to a whaler and get those furs and ivory to Marie. We need the money."

Cook and the Eskimos traversed the 400 miles to the "take-off" point, hunting musk oxen for provisions on the way. At Svartevoeg, around March 15, 1908 he sent back all but four of his Eskimos. Leaving the land, Cook covered about sixty miles in two days.

Establishing another storage cache, he sent two more Eski-mos and their sleds back to camp. Now it was Cook and his two native companions, Etukishook and Abwelah, two sledges and twenty six dogs. They pushed on for another thirty six days. On April 21, 1908, Dr. Cook, noting "the only pulsating creatures in a dead world of ice," claimed to have found the North Pole.

Cook made reckonings, notes and photographs. He left a small flag—the Stars and Stripes—on the ice, an exercise in futility for sure. The main thing now was to get back and announce the feat. It should be relatively easy to return in time to help Franke pack up.

On returning south, he did not know of, nor take into account, the prevailing southwestward drift. The three wandered past the advance point and its caches of supplies at Svartevoeg. He passed the land mass of Ellsmere Island and into the long winter's night they sledged. They holed up near Cape Sparbo for the 8-month darkness, lost to the world. The New York doctor and his two skilled companions survived in the long night. Cook's account of this struggle is unsurpassed in writing of cold, loneliness, despair, ingenuity, determination, the role of hope in survival and in the humanities of the three souls who came through it. It is also a great tale of the facts of life in the frozen expanse of the Arctic.

CHAPTER SIX

The race to the North Pole was not a race; it was never close. Almost a whole year passed between the two claimed successes. Due to the winter's long night, they both used the sun's rising to leave the land and move out onto the ice. They, no doubt, had learned that from the Eskimos—"The sun's up, let's move." Cook left Svartevoeg on March 18, 1908. Peary left Cape Sheridan on eastern Ellsmere Island on February 28, 1909. The race was really to get the news home for the big media event, which the quarrel became. Presenting the train of events in a divided sheet may help put the timing of events into proper perspective.

COOK	1907	PEARY
Meets Bradley. Plans.	March	Hoped to explore the North Pole this year. Delays in outfitting his ship, *Roosevelt*. Loss of backer, Jessup, further delays.

SS *Bradley* sails from Gloucester.	July	
Arrives at Etah. Eskimos, dogs camp at Annoatok.	Aug.	President Theodore Roosevelt launches his namesake ship.
Bradley returns to N.Y. Bridgman told of Pole attempt by Cook.	Sept.	Peary excited by Bridgman. Accuses Cook of sub-rosa Pole try.
Cook hunting, preparing sledges, training. Eskimos and dogs assembled.	Oct./ Nov./ Dec.	Preparations continue for expedition. Has official backing of government as well as business and educators.
	1908	
Franke and others back at Annoatok. Cook and two Eskimos leave land.	March 18	
Cook, Etukishook and Abwelah reach North Pole.	April 21	
Cook is lost on his return journey.	July 6	Peary sails on *Roosevelt*.

Franke has broken leg. Caches ivory and furs. Meets Peary at Etah.	Aug.	Peary at Etah. Complains to world—Cook has "stolen my Eskimos and dogs."
Trying to get to camp hits onset of winter near Cape Sparbo 200 miles southwest of Annoatok. Digs in.	Sept.	Refuses to let Franke take Cook's possessions on the return of his ship. Peary moves to base camp at Cape Columbia at top of Ellsmere.
Tales of wild living in frozen north—bears, birds, seals, wolves and weather.	Nov.	Hunting, assembling equipment for dash to Pole, 500 miles away. Assembles 2 explorers, 18 eskimos and 123 dogs. Superb plan for trek to Pole.
	1909	
Cook iced in.	Feb.	1st division takes off from land to cache supplies for return.

Cook moving toward camp.	April 1	Bartlett, next to last to leave camp, now returns.
Cook arrives at Annoatok; greeted by Whitney.	April 6	Peary, Henson and 4 Eskimos plant U.S. flag at North Pole.
Cook, with new sled and Eskimos, heads for Greenland. Leaves papers with Whitney.	April 19	
	April 26	Peary back at Cape Sheridan.
Cook reaches Upernavik.	May 21	Peary prepares to board *Roosevelt*.
On board the *Hans Egide* bound for Copenhagen.	Aug.	Perry at Etah. Sees Whitney and learns the lost Cook is alive. Questions Cook's Eskimos.

N.Y. Herald announces Cook's Polar success.	Sept. 2	
Arrives, as hero, in Copenhagen. Receives medal from Royalty.	Sept. 4	
	Sept. 9	Peary announces to world his reaching of the Pole on April 6, 1909.
Cook welcomed to N.Y.	Sept. 21	Peary in Nova Scotia.

CHAPTER SEVEN

Cook and his Eskimos, inspired by being alive after magic escapes from conditions of pure horror, finally came to Annoatok, 14 months after they left the camp. This voyage, this return trip from the Pole, must rank with the greatest feats of man on the ice. Cook had time, and took it, to produce voluminous notes. While he wrote, Atukishook and Abwelah sewed, sang and snoozed. In other moments, and as the need arose, they would kill animals with stones, or trap musk oxen with ropes. In their wisdom they hid from polar bears until the beasts hibernated. When the sun again appeared, like good natives they followed the shadow spirits with all possible haste, which was not outstanding, to Annoatok, 300 miles away. Sled dogs, long since gone, (dead and/or eaten) the three pulled the remaining cut-down sledge. At times they used a collapsible canoe for hunting and water travel.

Among those to greet the "ghosts" was Harry Whitney, a wealthy adventurer who had come north with Peary. He wanted to hunt, but didn't care to make the arduous Polar try. At the camp were two ship's stewards left to care for some of Peary's stores. They had also assumed charge of the box-like shanty that Cook and Franke had built there. Cook found a few things that Marie had sent him some months previous—knives, hatchets and a rare treat, butter. With these Cook could barter for a sledge and a way out to announce his feat.

Whitney washed and fed Cook, of whom he said, "This is the dirtiest white man I ever saw." Cook supervised his own eating, taking small amounts very frequently. He told Whitney they had reached the Pole but swore him to secrecy. He divided his voluminous notes, and asked Whitney to take them and his instruments home to Marie. Whitney tried to convince Cook to stay, recover his strength, and go back with him. But Cook was sure that by now Peary would have reached the Pole if he were ever to do so. It was important to announce his own feat before having a run-in with Peary.

Cook took off with two Eskimos on April 18, after only three days. They travelled by sledge, toward Greenland's southeast coast. He hoped to find a ship bound for Denmark, the nearest civilization whose connection with the rest of the world he needed. He waited at Apernavik to board the Danish ship, *Hans Egede*. The ship voyage was slow and agonizing. On September 1, 1909, as the ship made the Shetland Islands, Cook cabled the *New York Herald* his discovery of the North Pole. The following day the world knew it. Two days later the *Hans Egede* brought the doctor to an enthusiastic public and royal welcome in Copenhagen. He was greeted by a Prince, and given a gold medal commemorating his achievement.

The overwhelmed and weary Cook was sought out by W. T. Stead, who walked him through the ceremonies and managed the large and eager press. Getting Cook out of his greasy clothes and in attire fit to meet Royalty was easy for Stead, a skilled press agent.[3]

Peary had made an extraordinarily rapid return from the Pole to his base camp. By July he had come to Etah and learned that Cook was not dead, as he had expected, but alive and claiming to have been to the Pole. Peary was angry and disturbed. He refused to allow Whitney to transport Cook's belongings. They were left at Etah, where Peter Freuchen[4] later told of Eskimos taking the instruments as back-pay due them. Peary talked to Etukishook and Abwelah. He reported that the Eskimos claimed they and Cook had never left the land. Peary made his announcement from Labrador, stating that Cook had passed on a 'gold brick.' He would delay his return as he did not want a big welcome home until it was clear that Cook was a liar.

CHAPTER EIGHT

Media events are born in some bare facts, and nurtured by self-interests and the creation of controversy. This "let's you and him fight" was the leading event for more than a year. The irascible Peary was great copy with his propensity to be the "one, the ordained, the only one." And hadn't he paid the price? Almost a lifetime of strenuous effort, and "him with only two toes left." Cook, on the other hand, could—and did for a time—afford to be gallant with "room for us both" being a great line.

The sun of September 21, 1909 was up in New York harbor when dozens of tugs and other small boats carrying the press got to Cook at quarantine about 7 a.m. Explosive relief was Marie's reward for the long wait. She and her daughters, Ruth, 10, and Helene, 4, confused by the crush around their handsome father, nevertheless warmed his heart. His brothers pressed forward for a brief hug. Still embracing Marie, he faced the press as long as he could endure it. Ducking out they transferred to a side-wheeler, the *Grand Republic*, and with 500 admirers aboard, headed for Brooklyn. The vessel docked amid 10,000 cheering Brooklynites, and a grand parade of automobiles, garishly decorated, drove to a reception at the Bushwick Club. Among those missing at this patriotic outburst was Herbert Bridgman, Secretary of the Explorer's Club, erstwhile friend, guest and employee of the now-famous doctor. He was probably at that moment in close conversation with important people, brewing a campaign to discredit Cook and get Peary his long-sought, and hard-earned prize. Bridgman had caused the New York Mayor to not greet Cook in the harbor.

Press comments of the time included the testimony of a Cape Breton native, who had traveled with both of the explorers. To the question, "Who is the best man?" there was this reply:

Dr. Cook is a splendid character, a gentleman through and through. He gave professional services to natives, pulled teeth, dressed wounds and gave out drugs without reward or compensation. Both are plucky, have great endurance, and stamina. Lieutenant Peary is more reserved. He has the habit of discipline and the desire for conquest. In his mind, he owned the natives, the dogs, the horizon, and the glory.

That seems to be a great part of the story and the controversy. Cook was driven to perform a feat and then shine. Peary, it would seem, wanted to be first at the North Pole for reasons men die for, or might even kill for.

All sides—professors, politicians, conmen, crooks, editors, and show men—got into the act. Charges and counter-charges claimed the headlines in the New York press and the telegraphic services. Calm judgments could not be made. Rumors were automatically elevated to new headlines. Either the *New York Times* was ahead of its time, or looking off into the future. They used gossip and rumor, or a planted error to become news and lead to editorial support. The *Times* of that day did not cast the fearful power it throws today, but it gained circulation with its undiluted effort to discredit Cook, or to cover up the bad

side of Peary (which he had) with silence. The *New York
Herald* was in Cook's camp as he had favored it with the first
and early news (for a price, of course.) "All the news fit to
print" on the Polar controversy was highly selective.

Both explorers proved to be strong, determined, and tal-
ented men. Peary turned to writing a book, *To The North Pole*,
published in 1910. He seemed to avoid, successfully, the hus-
tler types who came at Cook. Peary had the support of powerful business and academic personages, and the backing of the
new but prestigious National Geographic Society. They
moved to have their man designated first to the Pole. Cook
hardly had the time to read a headline. He gave out stories to
the newspapers, wrote magazine articles, and took to the lecture circuit—St. Louis, Chicago, Philadelphia. He and Marie
could not remain in their home, nor he remain in the practice
of medicine. The demand for Cook was great, and his need and
desire to capitalize on the moment prevailed.

During the first two months after the return of Dr. Cook,
another and still unnoticed complaint was brewing in the
Explorer's Club. "Did Cook climb Mt. McKinley?" Bridgman
and other Peary supporters moved this question into the New
York press. The press acted like sharks moving in to attack a
victim wounded and bleeding in the water, frenzied and eager.
"Fake," they cried. "Prove yourself." The now harried and
busy Cook sought to do it, believing that he was certainly more
credible than the Montana blacksmith, Barrill, "holding $1,500
of New York bribe money in his pocket." Cook could not beat
the news game. As they moved from one witness to another,
Cook's wishes to prove otherwise, were held false or not subject to proof, at least. More controversy!

If this new charge of faking was not enough to knock Cook
off his once honored position, then,

How about his stealing a dictionary from a dying clergy-man a way back in 1899, when Doctor Cook was in Tierra del Fuego?"

This concoction was based on the presence of Cook's name on an obscure lexicon of native language. The attempt to try, sentence and punish the doctor with little if any proof had a short but Cook-damaging life. The charge was made, for example, that the author of the classic, *Through the First Antarctic Night*, had never been there.

The Cooks had left the Waldorf for a small hotel in the New York suburbs. They hired an advisor to put his notes together to send to Copenhagen as added proof of his claim, missing terribly the papers that were lost through Whitney's troubles. Cook assumed a disguise at this point. Confused and stressed almost to the point of despair, he fled to Montreal, and from there to Europe. He sent for Marie and she joined him in Algeciras. The continued their flight until they found rest in far-off Paraguay. A short recovery period passed, and Marie returned to the children. The doctor went to London.

Sun tanned, with blonde hair and blue eyes, he sported a large, yellowish moustache, and stood tall and full-chested. His bearing now spoke of resolve. In late summer, 1910, Peary came to speak in London. Cook, in disguise, attended the lecture close to the front, without detection. Seeing the now-Commodore moved Cook to further efforts to finish his book, *My Attainment of the Pole*. He told a reporter of the *New York World* that he had regained his strength and was coming home to get his due. At the first crack out of the box on his return, for a good price, he let the *Hampton* magazine print a disgraceful piece, later repudiated. Damned if Cook wasn't back, and immediately put on the defensive. It was another media-born legend on his life.

Peary's book, *To The North Pole*, published in 1910, had followed a number of Cook magazine and newspaper accounts. Cook's book, which appeared in 1911, seemed to say that the two explorers covered much of the same ice, and experienced the same aura and presences. If they did not both come to the same indescribable and indefinite point, then they both were close, or Peary had copied Cook's earlier accounts. Such remarks did nothing to quench the fires of the press, and even the passage of three quarters of a century has not improved the chances of putting the matter to rest, or so it would appear.

Dr. Cook was signed up by the Chautauqua Circuit and lectured all over the land. At every important audience, the opposition was there ahead of him with leaflets telling of "Cook's lies." He was hosted for several days by Thomas Edison in his Fort Myers, Florida home, with Henry Ford and John Muir. Some encouragement came when the tough-minded Ford told him to, "keep up your fight."

Keep it up he did. He generated much interest and a loyal following. They began to petition their Congressmen to review Cook's claims. As a hearing in Congress neared, Cook met an old Chicago medical friend, Frank Thompson, M.D. He was a man of means and a free-wheeling adventurer at heart. It was the right time for him to meet Cook, who was almost worn to a frazzle by the one-night stands of the waning lecture circuit. Confrontations with Peary's proponents and Cook's detractors were still and always a story for the local press. He was ready for something else. Even the hope he had in a good word from Congress, which he felt was thinly based, made him ready for some other romantic siren call. Thompson wanted to climb Mt. Everest in the far away Himalayas. Would Cook join him?

CHAPTER NINE

By this time Marie and the girls were used to a part-time father, even though not pleased with the long separations. Marie sensed the excitement as her husband spoke of escaping the lecture tour with Dr. Thompson picking up most of the cost. Ignoring the War then raging in Europe, this medical pair took off for Honolulu via San Francisco. They stayed with an old friend of Cook's, the German Consul.

They reboarded their ship. In the course of the long voyage they socialized with some Indian officials who were homeward bound. On reaching Malaya, Cook and Thompson were arrested by the British Secret Service. What had the two heard when staying with the enemy German in Honolulu? To make matters worse, why were they fraternizing with Indian nationals, who were suspected of arms smuggling to an anti-British faction in India? It took time to clear the charges, which was done, but the authorities nixed any plan of the American doctors to go near the Himalayas.

The two took an extended vacation in Borneo and sailed among the South Seas for a few more months. As World War I drew closer to the United States, a way to sail home dried up. They tried Manila and Yokohama for berths to home. Casual shipping just wasn't available. They got passage to Siberia and made the long rail voyage to Copenhagen. Using their medical credentials (and probably Cook's earlier Danish fame, if any was left) they signed as ship's surgeons on a Danish liner and were home in New York on January 26, 1916. Whether either was helpful, medically or otherwise, on this winter cruise in the time of very active, able U-boats is not of record. The *Lusitania* was sunk in that ocean a short while later.

CHAPTER TEN

Now what to do? There was a 10-year hiatus in his once busy medical practice. The lecture circuit was worn threadbare after more than five years. Marie still had a modest fortune, and income from his books was not completely exhausted. He sat now in New York, 46 years old, in good physical health, but feeling unattached in almost all ways—to people and to things. He had not long to wait for action.

Dr. Thompson had returned to Chicago where, in addition to his practice, he was interested in new businesses and speculations. He needed a friend to go out and take an independent look at some oil properties in Wyoming; someone he could depend on, someone who had a good mind and nothing to sell. Cook went to Wyoming, found the property to be not worth Thompson's investment, but got excited by what he saw of the oil game. He stayed. He liked what he learned and, with Thompson's backing, a small oil exploration company was set up. The family moved west.

Ever the one to hear the bruit of fate tempting, he sold out his part of the firm and, smelling the oilier and richer fields of Texas, he moved southward. His age prevented his doing military duty. Manpower shortages caused by the call to arms opened places to put his efforts. He formed a new company and it bombed. He hired out as an explorer, working for a time for Tex Rickard of boxing fame (Jack Dempsey's manager). In a short while he was back in business for himself, and there was nothing small about the next effort.

He merged more than 400 failing or defunct oil companies into the Petroleum Producers Association of Fort Worth, Texas. He rented a floor of a bank as offices, hired 95 stenographers, and sent out a prospectus offering stock for sale. He travelled all over the southwest, often with his teenage daughter, Helene, in a dusty twin six Packard. His hair was now greying, his sturdy body a bit paunchy, and his appearance not so rugged as in his Arctic days.

Cook moved into a fast crowd and most probably knew that for sure when he had encountered Tex Rickard. The war was over, and with the lack of the armed contest to heat up the economy, the fast buck was getting harder to run down. Deals were being made. In April 1922, Senator Hendrick of Wyoming asked the Secretary of the Interior, Albert B. Fall, "if the lease Harry Sinclair had on the oil fields at Teapot Dome had been cleared with the U. S. Navy, since the Senate had given that oil to them?"

What a question!

Word of this probe reached the sensitive ears of President Warren Harding, then touring far-away Alaska territory. It never was clearly shown to what extent the President's death was due to food poisoning or to the Teapot Dome scandal. Heads began to roll at high levels. The sweep of the crusade to clean up the ranks of oil men caught several hundred in Texas.

Peary had died in 1920 of pernicious anemia and complications. (Cook was the first to make this diagnosis when he went to help Peary in 1901.) The Polar controversy had the good manners to suffer fatigue and anemia as well, but it was not dead. Herbert Houston, a fitting successor to Herbert Bridgman, when told of the results of an investigation into Texas oil fields by an agent of his "National Vigilance Committee" exclaimed, "We have discovered an old friend, Dr. Cook. He did not discover the North Pole, but we have discovered him."

Cook was visited by a Postal Inspector. He turned over accounts the Government wanted to examine. While working in Little Rock he learned of a warrant for his arrest and he returned to Fort Worth. Apparently aware of the coming trouble, he had worked out a divorce with Marie that protected her own small fortune from involvement in the troubles. A news story of his having illegal whiskey and a visiting female in a Texas hotel room did little more than make a brief appearance and was not part of the divorce. (In all his agonies, alcohol never showed as a fault in the doctor's character, and rarely, if ever, a dame.)

He surrendered to the District Attorney in Fort Worth in April 1923, charged along with 13 associates for having used the mails to defraud, exaggerating the prospectus of their company and overpromoting the sales of stock. His associates copped pleas for light jail sentences. Cook, alone, felt he could establish the worth of the holdings, even though the current market value was badly depressed due, not in the least, to the aura of scandal. He hoped to escape jail, and refused to plea bargain. He went to trial in October 1923. He gambled, he lost. The sitting judge, full of accounts of Cook's notoriety, showed him no mercy. On November 20, the doctor was found guilty and given a harsh sentence: 14 years and nine months in prison and a $12,000 fine.

Marie, though divorced, attended the trials. She and Helene brought food and favors to him as he languished in custody, trying to maintain his spirits. She did raise funds for an appeal which he also lost. He stayed in the Fort Worth jail for almost 500 days.

CHAPTER ELEVEN

On April 6, 1925, the 16th anniversary of Robert Peary's claim at the North Pole, Dr. Cook entered the U. S. Penitentiary at Leavenworth, Kansas.

His first days at Leavenworth were rough. He refused any visitors. As his letters showed, his hand was not firm; he was not well, at least mentally. In spite of a long lapse from things medical, he was made night supervisor of the prison hospital. This was still uninspiring, but with no place to go he turned his mind to creating. He wrote in the prison publication *New Era* on conditions of man; good essays on alcohol and drug abuse. At assemblies he often spoke of things that took the prisoners' only travelling parts, their minds, on trips into the Polar ice, north and south; of stories of brave men the inmates would never see; of animals they may have never heard of.

The time was long. For a man who had used his freedom to go to the ends of the earth he had to do mentally stimulating things to keep freedom a viable concept. He found the way.

His greatest day in prison was the occasion when Roald Amundsen, his *Belgira* companion, and now a respected and world-famous man, got off a train and came a hard route to Leavenworth on his own. In the warden's office they talked at length of other times. Amundsen told the press, "Dr. Cook may not have discovered the Pole, but Commodore Peary may not have either. The former has as good a claim as the latter."

For this, Amundsen, discoverer of the South Pole and the Northwest Passage to the North Pole, experienced cancellation by the National Geographic Society of a lecture he had contracted to give.

At the termination of his prison sentence, a speaker at a banquet inside the walls said, "never a prisoner who did so much good as Fred Cook." Shortly before his time expired, a magazine wanted to buy a story if he would not mention a claim for the North Pole. Cook refused. He needed money, but "not that badly." He left prison in a two-piece dark suit, an old felt hat on his head. In the pocket of the dingy looking coat he had $50, courtesy of the U. S. Prison Service. A picture of him boarding a Kansas City train showed a moderately heavy man, with a prominent nose, soft, sad-dog looking eyes in a fleshy face. But on his face was half a smile, surely saying how he felt about the free air. He did not look like he was bound for either Pole, high mountains, or the Chautauqua circuit. He left prison on March 8, 1930.

He went to Chicago, where he checked in with Dr. Frank Thompson, his old friend, and now his parole contact, whom he continued to visit. He got a small spiritual lift when the Boy Scouts of Chicago gave him an honor. Getting his head up he headed eastward to his daughter's home near Buffalo, New York. He was by no means the cocky, jaunty, self-assured doctor of the turn of the century. He was an old man who, for another decade, would answer requests by churches, community gatherings, and schools, by recounting tales of his fabulous adventures. He felt moved to help Helene clean the house and to do the dishes. He worked without speed on his book *Return*

From the Pole, depending on the voluminous notes that he had kept safe.

He missed very few targets as he sued people who had wronged him right and left. He won not a single case. He appealed to the American Geographical Society to review his Polar claims. "Sorry, no funds." He had a visit from a later explorer, Sir Hubert Wilkins, who talked with Cook of his desire to try for the Pole by submarine. Late in his life, Rudolph Franke, on whom once so much depended to get the furs and ivory home from Etah, came by and spoke a few words in Eskimo to his old boss.

In May 1940, Dr. Cook was a guest in the home of his long-time friend, Ralph Shainwold. Ralph had been a companion on the trip around McKinley in 1903, the only American friend to meet him in Copenhagen and through all the times, good and bad, a kind of friend who never wavered. Ralph's wife was terminally ill and to her went the last ministry of Cook's profession. While on this visit he suffered a cerebral hemorrhage on May 3.

Now Shainwald helped care for him as more than a kind and old friend. He secured from President Franklin Roosevelt a full pardon, and the old doctor was alert enough to murmur, "Thanks."

On August 5, 1940 Frederick Albert Cook died in a hospital in New Rochelle, New York. The triumphs, errors, and the calumnies washed over him never seemed to overcome the spirit within this man, revealed in the dedication page of his *My Attainment of the Pole*.

TO THE PATHFINDERS

To the Indian who invented pemmican and snowshoes
To the Eskimo who gave the art of sled travelling
To this twin family of wild folk who have no flag

Goes the first credit.
To the forgotten trailmakers whose book of experience
has been a guide.
To the fallen victors whose bleached bones mark steps
in the ascent of the ladder of latitude
To these, the pathfinders, past, present and future
I inscribe the first page.
In the ultimate success there is glory enough to go
around.

Any way he can be cut up in pieces and put back, he was one
hell of a man. If the peculiar polar buffs didn't or wouldn't put
him in their shrine, it would seem that the medical profession
could acclaim him a good doctor.

FOOTNOTES.

[1]This was evidence of Cook's diagnostic acumen as this disease was only to be explained 25 years later as a dietary deficiency condition.

[2]Surviving business the well-known Abercrombie and Fitch.

[3]I would not have known Stead from "Adam's off-ox" had I not done a story on Leander Starr Jamison, M. D. for this opus. Stead seemed to make the world a small place, even then. It was Stead who, at the climax of a large banquet in Cook's honor at Copenhagen, read a telegram announcing that Robert Peary, U.S.N. had lay the Stars and Stripes at the foot of the pole on April 6, 1909. Cook's remarks praising Peary were deemed gracious by the throngs, for as he said, "There was plenty of glory for both of us."

[4]Freuchen, a polar explorer himself, speaking of the two rivals said, "Cook was a gentleman and a liar; Peary was neither."

BIBLIOGRAPHY

Cook, F. A. *Through the First Antarctic Night.* Doubleday and McClure, 1900.

Cook, F. A. *My Attainment of the Pole.* Polar, 1911.

Carnes, Hugh. *Winner Lose All.* Little, Brown, 1973.

Freeman, Andrew. *The Case for Dr. Cook.* Coward-McCann, 1961.

Gibbons, Russell W. *An Enigma in Polar History.* Dartmouth College Library, 1968.

Hunt, Wm. R. *To Stand at the Pole.* Stein and Day, 1981.

McMillan, Donald B. *How Peary Reached the Pole.* Houghton Mifflin, 1934.

Special thanks to Janet Vetter (Cook's granddaughter) and Russell Gibbons for other valuable data.

How You Can Keep Informed On Important Issues . . . While Catering To Your Funny Bone's Needs

At the *American Spectator*, we still have fun providing you with keen political analysis, investigative journalism, and a thoughtful defense of the best of our cultural heritage. It's a trend dating back to 1967, when the magazine was founded as an anti-radical journal by students at Indiana University. The youthful exuberance and biting wit of its writers soon made the *American Spectator* a national publication, and we have strived to keep up the levity to this day.

The *American Spectator* publishes information ignored by today's mainstream media. Each monthly issue brings articles with viewpoints and analyses refreshingly at odds with the conventional wisdom, some tongue-in-cheek, some deadly serious. Here's your opportunity to receive provocative articles on a monthly basis, along with book and film reviews . . . humor . . . Americana . . . foreign reporting . . . saloon reviews (you read that right) . . . all from such luminaries as Fred Barnes, Tom Bethell, Victor Gold, Brit Hume, Robert Novak, Joe Queenan, Benjamin J. Stein, and the *American Spectator*'s founder and editor, R. Emmett Tyrrell, Jr.

◆ ◆ ◆

What They Say:

"Our nation's intellectual life would be more than a little poorer without the *American Spectator* surveying the scene."
—President George Bush

"Even those who dislike the conservative politics espoused by the *American Spectator* have to admit that the monthly can be awfully amusing." —*USA Today*

" . . . rapidly growing impact in Washington among the policy elite." —Hon. Jack Kemp

N ow you may take advantage of this special no-risk trial offer for *Call Me A Doctor* readers—only $19.95 for ten monthly issues of the *American Spectator* (that's more than $10 off the newsstand price).

To order more copies of Jack Griffitts' *Call Me A Doctor*, send $17.95 ($15.95 plus $2.00 postage and handling) to:

The American Spectator
P.O. Box 549
Arlington, Virginia 22216-0549

Bulk discount of 50% on orders of ten copies or more.